Dogs and puppies

My First Fun
Animal
Questions
and Answers

My First Fun
Animal
Questions
and Answers

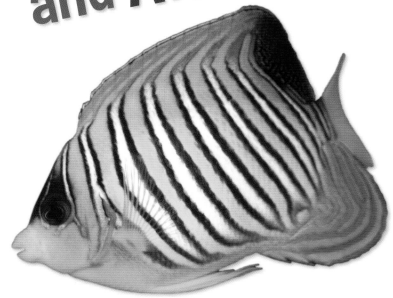

Camilla de la Bedoyere, Anna Claybourne,
Jinny Johnson and Barbara Taylor

Miles
KeLLY

First published in 2011 by Miles Kelly Publishing Ltd
Harding's Barn, Bardfield End Green, Thaxted, Essex, CM6 3PX, UK

This edition published 2014

4 6 8 10 9 7 5

Publishing Director Belinda Gallagher
Creative Director Jo Cowan
Editor Claire Philip
Cover Designer Simon Lee
Designers Kayleigh Allen, Greg Best, Andrew Crowson, Sally Lace,
Phil Morash at Fineline Studios, Rocket Design Ltd,
Andrea Slane, Liz Wiffen at Punch Bowl Design
Image Manager Liberty Newton
Indexer Gill Lee
Production Manager Elizabeth Collins
Reprographics Stephan Davis, Jennifer Cozens, Anthony Cambray
Assets Lorraine King
Character Cartoonist Mike Foster

ISBN 978-1-78209-573-6

Printed in China

British Library Cataloguing-in-Publication Data
A catalogue record for this book is available from the British Library

Made with paper from a sustainable forest

www.mileskelly.net
info@mileskelly.net

contents

Are dogs and puppies friendly?

**Most pet dogs and puppies are tame –
this means they are friendly and like to
be around people.** There are more
than 200 types, or breeds,
of dogs such as pointers,
which are clever and
easily trained.

Pointer puppies

What do dogs eat?

Newborn puppies drink their mother's milk. As they get older, dogs eat meat and special biscuits. Their food contains vitamins that help them grow strong and healthy. Dogs need plenty of fresh water every day.

Burmese mountain dog

Dog biscuits

Chew

Fresh water

Messy pup!

Some dogs love to get mucky. They'll roll around in stinky mud or jump into dirty water for a quick dip!

Do toy dogs love to play?

Toy dogs are small dogs. They love to play with children who hold them carefully and treat them well. Yorkshire Terriers (also known as Yorkies), Chihuahuas and Pugs are toy dogs and they make great family pets.

Measure
Some toy dogs are only 20 centimetres tall. Use a ruler to find out how big this is.

Yorkshire Terrier

can I have a pet wolf?

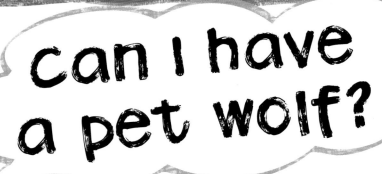

No – it would be too dangerous! Wolves are the largest type of wild dog, and they aren't tame. Grey wolves live in family groups called packs that hunt together and look for animals to eat.

Grey wolf mother and cubs

Are all baby dogs called puppies?

No, young wild dogs such as dingoes and foxes are called cubs. Dingoes live in Australia and foxes, such as the red fox, live in many parts of the world.

Fox cub

itchy and scratchy!

Tiny jumping bugs called fleas can set up home in a dog's fur. Fleas make dogs itch, so they scratch.

Think

When people come to your home, how does your family make them feel welcome?

Why are postmen scared of dogs?

A dog likes to guard its home, or territory, so if a stranger, such as a postman, comes into its territory a dog might bark. Not all dogs bark as a warning – sometimes they are just happy to see you!

what is a litter?

'Litter' is the word for a group of puppies born at the same time. A mother dog is usually pregnant for about two months, as the puppies grow inside her. Most mother dogs have litters of three to eight puppies at a time and take care of them for the first few weeks of their lives.

Paint
Draw your family and some dogs that look like them. Then add colour with paints.

Mother dog

Are dogs helpful?

Dogs can help people in many ways. Guide dogs are trained to help people who have difficulty seeing, hearing or walking. These dogs can warn their owners of danger and guide them safely when they go out.

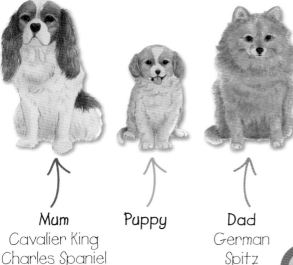

Mum
Cavalier King
Charles Spaniel

Puppy

Dad
German
Spitz

Litter of
Dachshund
puppies

Do all puppies look like their parents?

Not if the mother and father dog are different breeds. Puppies may have features from both parents – long ears from their Mum, for example, and fluffy fur from their Dad.

Dogs in space!

In 1960, two dogs called Strelka and Belka were sent into space by astronauts – they landed home safely.

How smart are dogs?

Border collie

Some dogs are much smarter than others. The cleverest dogs can be trained to work with people. Collies are trained to herd sheep on farms. They also protect the sheep from animals that might hunt them, such as foxes.

can dogs and puppies swim?

Some puppies learn to swim as soon as they can run, while others never learn. When dogs and puppies swim, they move as though they are running underwater – this is known as the doggy paddle.

Alaskan malamute

Swim

When you next go swimming, practise doing the doggy paddle.

soggy doggy!

Basset hounds find swimming in water very difficult because they have such short legs!

Do dogs look like their owners?

That's a matter of opinion! It is true that some tall, thin people own dogs that are long and thin – and some short, broad people have short, broad dogs. However, most dogs and their owners look very different from one another.

Why do dogs chase balls?

It is natural for dogs to chase things that move, especially balls. They do this because pet dogs are related to wild dogs, which have to catch food to eat. Dogs are playful animals too, and chasing balls is fun!

Dog chasing a ball

what's up!

Healthy dogs have much better hearing than humans. They react to sounds that are very far away.

can dogs have stripes?

Dogs come in many colours, but none have stripes! Dalmatians are known for their white coats and black spots. The puppies are born completely white — their spots develop after a few weeks.

Walt Disney's
101 Dalmatians

Do old dogs turn grey?

Yes — the fur around their muzzles turns grey or white. Some elderly dogs also have hearing problems. Old dogs have less energy than young puppies and so they sleep a lot more.

Paint

Draw a picture of how you think you will look when you are grown-up.

Elderly dog

How do dogs keep warm?

Saint Bernard

Most dogs have thick fur coats to keep out the cold. Saint Bernards are suited to very cold climates. They are large, strong dogs bred to rescue lost travellers in snowy mountains.

Happy holiday!
If you take a pet dog abroad they will need their own 'pet passport'. It shows they are fit and healthy.

which puppies have wrinkles?

The wrinkliest puppies are Shar Peis. They have deep folds of skin around their heads, faces and bodies. As they get older, Shar Peis grow into their wrinkles, but even the adults are still very wrinkly around their heads.

Shar Pei puppies

Make
Design a poster showing some animals that can survive in very cold places.

Are dogs colour-blind?

Dogs can see colours — but not in the same way we do. Guide dogs can't tell the difference between red, amber and green in a traffic light. They look at the brightness and position of a light to know when it is safe to cross.

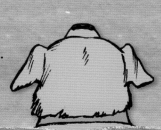

why do puppies chew?

Puppies chew when they are teething (growing new teeth). It can make their gums sore and chewing helps them feel better. Dogs also like to chew toys when they are playing.

Labrador puppy

Why do dogs fetch?

Hunting dogs were trained to fetch game birds, such as pheasants, that had been caught by their owners whilst hunting. Now most of these types of dogs, such as retrievers, are kept as pets. They still love to play fetch!

Golden retriever

Imagine
Make up a story about a sausage dog. What is its name, and what mischief does it get up to?

When is a dog like a sausage?

When it's a sausage dog! This type of dog has a very long body and four short legs. The proper name is 'Dachshund', which means 'badger dog'. Dachshunds are very good at digging.

Top dog!
A long time ago, a dog ruled the country of Norway. It was king for three years and signed important papers with a paw print!

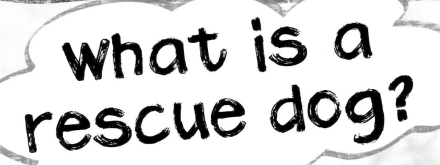

what is a rescue dog?

Rescue dogs are trained to find people who are lost or trapped. These dogs use their strong sense of smell to follow a person's trail. They can even find people who are trapped under snow.

Chow chow

Do all dogs have pink tongues?

Not all dogs – Chow Chows have blue-black tongues. The insides of their mouths are blue-black too. These dogs have been bred in China for thousands of years and are very loyal to their owners.

Alsatian
rescue dog

Sniff the whiff!

Dogs have such a strong sense of smell they can smell fresh food long before they can see it.

Hello

When you greet a friend how do you show that you are happy to see them? Do you shake hands?

when can puppies wag their tails?

Puppies usually start to wag their tails when they are about four weeks old and still feeding on their mother's milk. Older dogs wag their tails when they are excited to see another dog, or a person they like.

Are puppies born blind?

Newborn puppies are born blind and totally helpless. They first open their eyes when they are about nine days old. At three weeks of age, puppies can move around clumsily. At six weeks old they begin to eat solid food.

Newborn puppy

Two weeks old

Sloppy doggy!

When some dogs see a plate of food their mouths fill up with saliva, which sometimes dribbles out of their mouths. It's called 'drooling'.

Three weeks old

How do hot dogs cool down?

Panting

Dogs pant when they need to cool down. When we get too hot we can sweat, and take off some clothes. Dogs can't take off their thick, warm fur and they can only sweat from their paws. Panting helps them keep cool and comfortable.

Talk

Ask your Mum or Dad about the ways you have changed since you were a baby.

Why do puppies sleep so much?

When puppies are awake they are busy learning, playing and feeding. It tires them out quickly. As they grow, puppies spend less time snoozing.

Five weeks old

Eight weeks old

why do dogs love to sniff?

Dogs have a much better sense of smell than we do. They like to sniff things because smells, or scents, tell them a lot about the world around them. They can even recognize people and other dogs by their scents.

Basset hound

Pretend

Imagine you are following a trail. Use your eyes, ears and sense of smell to find your way.

can dogs sense danger?

Dogs often react to sudden movements or loud noises. It means they are alert to possible dangers. Some dogs can even sense earthquakes and thunderstorms before they happen.

Bad fur day!

The fur of Hungarian Puli dogs grows down to the ground. It needs brushing every day so it doesn't get too knotted.

Huskies pulling sleigh

which is the strongest dog?

Huskies are one of the strongest dog breeds. They live in cold places and are strong enough to cope with freezing weather while pulling heavy sleds.

Do dogs have haircuts?

Long-haired dogs need haircuts to keep them cool. It can be very dangerous for dogs to overheat and lots of fur keeps in warmth. Short-haired dogs shed their fur throughout the year, mostly in the spring and summer.

Chocolate poodles

can dogs talk to each other?

Dogs 'talk' to each other and to us by barking. Loud, non-stop barking usually means that a dog is worried about something. Two or three short barks are a dog's way of saying 'Hello'.

Brittany spaniel

Nice to meet you

Dogs and puppies are friendly creatures and can live alongside other pets happily – as long as they are properly introduced.

why do puppies need exercise?

Exercise is good for puppies and dogs. It keeps them healthy and strong, and uses up energy so they sleep well. Exercise is also a type of play, which makes dogs and puppies happy — without it they can become restless.

Exercise
Riding bikes and playing in parks are fun ways to get some exercise.

Do big ears help dogs hear?

Not if they are long and floppy, like a bloodhound's. These dogs have a fantastic sense of smell but their large, droopy ears can cause hearing problems and even deafness.

Bad breath!

Dogs can have bad breath and gum disease, just like us! Owners should brush their dog's teeth with toothpaste made specially for dogs.

Bloodhound

Do dogs like being brushed?

Some dogs like being brushed, but others hate it! Brushing a dog is called 'grooming' and it helps to keep their fur clean and tidy. Samoyeds have beautiful white coats, and most of them like their long, thick fur being brushed.

Samoyed

How big do dogs grow?

A dog's size depends on its breed. Some dogs, such as Great Danes, grow very tall and can measure more than 80 centimetres from the floor to their shoulder. Chihuahuas are one of the smallest breeds of dog. They can be just 15 centimetres tall.

Great Dane

Discover

Use a measuring tape to see how tall a Great Dane can be.

Chihuahua

can puppies be trained?

Cardboard box bed

Puppies are eager to learn, so they can be easily trained. As they grow, puppies learn to recognize their own names and how to follow commands. They also need to be house-trained, which means going outside to go to the toilet.

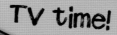

TV time!

Some dogs will sit and watch the bright lights and moving images on TV screens. They don't understand what they see, but seem to like it!

34

Do puppies go to the doctor?

Puppies need to see a vet if they are unwell. A vet is an animal doctor. All dogs and puppies need to visit the vet so they can be given vaccinations to keep them healthy.

Vet examining a puppy

Play

Pretend you are a vet, and you have a surgery full of unwell pets to look after.

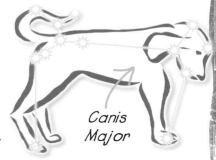

Canis Minor

Canis Major

When is a dog a star?

When it is in the sky! Groups of stars are called constellations and two of them are named after dogs. One is called *Canis Major*, or Bigger Dog, and the other one is *Canis Minor*, or Smaller Dog.

Quiz time

Do you remember what you have read about dogs and puppies? Here are some questions to test your memory. The pictures will help you. If you get stuck, read the pages again.

3. What is a litter?

page 14

4. Do old dogs turn grey?

page 19

1. What do dogs eat?

page 11

5. Which puppies have wrinkles?

page 21

2. Why are postmen scared of dogs?

page 13

6. Are dogs colour-blind?

page 21

7. Why do puppies chew?

page 22

11. Can dogs talk to each other?

page 31

12. Can puppies be trained?

page 34

8. When can puppies wag their tails?

page 25

9. Are puppies born blind?

page 26

13. When is a dog a star?

page 35

10. Can dogs sense danger?

page 29

Answers

1. Meat and special biscuits
2. Because dogs bark to protect their territory
3. A group of puppies born at the same time
4. Yes, some fur turns grey or white
5. Shar Pei puppies
6. No, they just see colour differently to us
7. They chew because their gums are sore or during play
8. When they are around four weeks old
9. Yes, puppies only open their eyes when they are around nine days old
10. Yes, some even sense thunderstorms and earthquakes
11. Yes, but by barking – not with words
12. Yes, puppies are eager to learn
13. When it's a star constellation, such as *Canis Minor*

37

cats and kittens

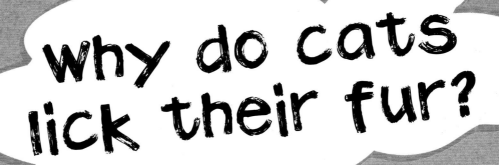

why do cats lick their fur?

Cats lick their fur to keep themselves clean.
A cat's tongue has a rough surface, which helps to remove dirt, loose fur and small insect pests. A mother cat will lick her kittens to clean them and to bond with them.

Mother cat

Kitten

what do cats and kittens eat?

Cats are carnivores, which means they eat meat. Wild cats have to hunt other animals to eat. Pet cats and kittens eat special food made for cats, as well as meat and fish.

Kitten

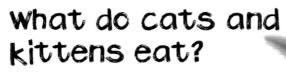

Food bowl

How does a cat show it's angry?

An angry or frightened cat arches its back and makes its fur stand on end. This makes the cat look bigger than it really is and helps to warn off enemies.

Playtime!

When a cat plays with a toy mouse it's not just having fun, it is practising how to hunt a real one!

41

why do kittens play?

Kittens play because it's fun! It's also good exercise and helps them to grow stronger. From four weeks old, kittens start to play. Play-fighting with their litter mates helps kittens learn how to get on with other animals.

Kittens playing with a ball of wool

How long do cats sleep?

Cats sleep for about 16 hours a day! Many cats rest during the day and are most active early in the morning and at night. Sleep is extra important for kittens because it helps them to grow.

Sleeping cats

Think
Work out how many hours you sleep at night. Do you have more or less sleep than a cat?

What makes cats itch?

A cat that keeps scratching itself might have fleas. These are tiny insects that live on animals. Fleas feed on an animal's blood, and their bite is very itchy. A cat with fleas should be seen by a vet.

Flea

Cats win!
Cats are the most popular pets. There are about eight million pet cats in the UK and six million pet dogs.

HOW do cats carry their kittens?

Cats can't pick their kittens up with her paws, so they use their mouths. To carry her kitten, a mother cat holds the loose skin on its neck. This is called the 'scruff' and it doesn't hurt the kitten when it is carried like this.

A mother cat carrying her kitten

why do cats purr?

Cats usually purr when they are feeling happy and content. The noise comes from the breathing muscles in the cat's chest. If you put your hand on a loudly purring cat you can feel the vibrations of the sound.

Purring cat →

Speedy cat!
A pet cat can run at about 50 kilometres an hour. Cheetahs are the fastest wild cats and can run at twice this speed.

Are black cats witches' cats?

No, of course not! Many years ago some people believed that black cats were witches in disguise and that they helped witches to carry out their magic.

Purr
Practise making a purring sound. Relax your tongue, curl the end up a little and breathe out.

can cats and dogs be friends?

Yes, especially if they first meet when they are young. If a kitten and puppy grow up together they can get on very well. However an older dog may chase cats, and a cat will often hiss or swipe its claws at a dog.

Puppy

Kitten

where did pet cats come from?

All pet cats probably came from a kind of cat called the wildcat. This cat still lives in the wild in Scotland, other parts of Europe, Africa and Asia. It looks like a pet tabby cat, but it is slightly larger.

Wildcat

Stick

Find pictures of cats in magazines and papers. Stick them on a piece of paper to make a collage.

Give me a home!

Lots of cats are made homeless by owners who don't want them any more. Rescue centres look after them and try to find the cats new homes.

why do cats eat grass?

Eating grass helps a cat to cough up any loose fur that it has swallowed when cleaning itself. Grass also helps a cat to bring up bits of unwanted food, such as mouse bones and fur!

Fur ball

what do kittens drink?

Kittens drink their mother's milk for the first few weeks of their lives. A mother cat has teats, or nipples, on her tummy and her kittens suck on these to get milk. After four weeks, a kitten starts to drink water instead of milk.

Kittens suckling

Are cats good climbers?

Yes, cats are very good at climbing. They can scramble up anything that they can grip onto. Cats hang on with their sharp, strong claws and pull themselves up. Young cats sometimes have trouble getting back down again!

Cats climbing a tree →

clever cat!

Cats are very clever animals. They can even learn to open doors by pulling down handles with their paws.

HOW long do cats live?

Most pet cats live to between 12 and 15 years old. Some reach the age of 20 years old — that's nearly 100 in human years! One of the oldest cats ever lived to the age of 38.

Find out

Can you think of some other animals that are super climbers like cats?

How fast do kittens grow?

Kittens grow very quickly. They are born helpless — unable to see, hear or walk. By one week old their eyes open, and at four weeks they can run around. At eight weeks, kittens can eat solid food and are almost ready for life without their mother.

Newborn

One week old

Three weeks old

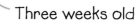
Eight weeks old

Four weeks old

Kitten's paw

HOW many toes do cats have?

Cats have 18 toes. They have five toes on each front paw and four toes on each back paw. Sometimes a kitten can be born with seven toes on one paw!

cat flap!

Many cats have their own special doors in and out of their owners' houses. Some can only be opened by a computer chip on the cat's collar.

why do cats wear collars?

So that people know they have owners. A collar can carry a telephone number so that if the cat gets lost, it can be brought back home. Some collars also help to get rid of fleas.

Make

Ask an adult to help you make a cat mask. Stick straws on a paper plate for whiskers, cut eyeholes and paint it.

Are there wild cats in the jungle?

A wild cat, called the jungle cat, lives in hot, wet forests in Asia. It hunts for rats, birds and fish along riverbanks and in swamps. Lots of other cats live in the wild, including big cats such as tigers.

Jungle cat

Do all cats have long tails?

Manx

No, they don't. There is a kind of cat called the Manx that does not have a tail at all. Another kind of cat called the Bobtail has only a very short stumpy tail – like a rabbit's tail.

Find out
Apart from tigers, can you name five other big cats? Use books and the Internet to help you.

How many kittens are in a litter?

Most mother cats give birth to four to six kittens at once – this is called a litter. Sometimes there can be as many as 12 kittens in a litter!

cat's eyes!
Cats have very good eyesight. They can see well at night – six times better than we can.

Do cats visit the doctor?

Yes, cats sometimes need to go to see an animal doctor called a vet. They are taken to the vet if they are ill, but also to have injections called vaccinations. These protect them from serious illnesses, such as 'cat flu'.

Vet examining a cat

Owner

Do cats like being picked up?

Some do, but some really don't. You should be careful when picking up a cat. Move slowly and calmly, and handle the cat gently. If it is not yours, check with the cat's owner first.

Lap lap!

A cat drinks by curling its tongue into a spoon shape and scooping up a little liquid at a time. It flicks water into its mouth and swallows every few laps.

Why does a cat rub its head on things?

To spread its scent. A cat will rub its head on its owner, or on furniture and other objects around its home. This marks out the cat's home area and warns other cats to stay away.

Play

Collect some sticks and pebbles and use them to mark out your own territory, or area, in your garden.

Cat rubbing its head against a chair

How many kinds of cat are there?

Russian Blue

There are more than 100 different kinds, or breeds, of pet cat. Each breed has certain features, such as a particular fur colour and pattern, body shape or eye colour. Some breeds weigh twice as much as others!

Longhair

Cornish Rex

what does a cat's meow mean?

Meowing is a cat's way of getting attention. A cat may meow to tell you it wants to be fed, stroked or let outside. A loud howl may mean a cat is in pain or upset. An owner quickly gets to understand the sounds their cat makes.

claws out!

Cats have super-sharp claws. They are perfect for grabbing hold of wriggly prey, such as a mouse, during a chase.

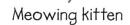

Meowing kitten

what is the cheshire cat?

The Cheshire Cat is a character in the book *Alice in Wonderland*, written by Lewis Carroll. It is best known for its big smile. Alice sees the cat sitting in a tree. Then it slowly disappears, leaving just its wide grin, which vanishes last.

create

Paint a picture of your own cat breed. Choose the colour and pattern you like and give your breed a name.

what does a new cat need?

It is a good idea to get a basic kit for your new pet. This should include bowls for water and food, cat food, and a litter (toilet) tray until the cat is old enough to go outside. Owners may also buy some toys, a brush and a bed for their pet.

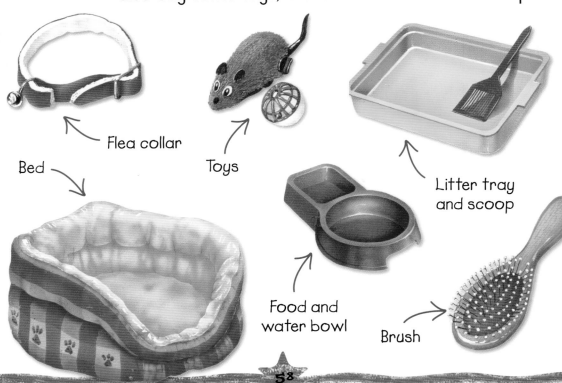

Flea collar

Bed

Toys

Litter tray and scoop

Food and water bowl

Brush

Do cats really have nine lives?

No, they don't. But sometimes it seems that cats can survive dangers that other animals can't. This is because a cat has excellent senses, strong muscles, good balance and super-fast reactions.

Tight squeeze!

A cat's whiskers are very sensitive. They help a cat judge whether its body will fit through a narrow space.

Make

Scrunch up some paper and tie it on some string to make a toy for your cat to chase.

Black cat

Are black cats really lucky?

Some people believe black cats are lucky, but others think they bring bad luck! Some people think that if a black cat crosses a person's path and walks away, it takes the person's good luck with it!

How high can a cat jump?

A cat can jump up to five times its height! Even a champion human high jumper can only jump a little higher than his or her own height. A cat's bendy body and the powerful muscles in its legs allow it to leap so far.

Cat jumping high in the air

Pretend

Imagine you are a cat. See how quietly you can creep up on something – perhaps your own cat!

why do cats bring presents?

No one knows exactly why cats bring mice or other creatures to their owners. Mother cats bring prey for their kittens. Maybe cats bring gifts to show their owners that they think of them as part of their family.

Know that nose!

All cats have a pattern of ridges on their nose. Like a person's fingerprints, no two cats have exactly the same pattern.

Are all cats furry?

Most are, but there is one kind of hairless cat called the Sphynx. It looks like it doesn't have any fur at all, but it is covered in very fine fur, called downy hair, which is thicker on the tail and legs.

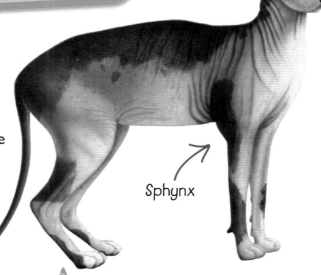

Sphynx

Does a cat 'talk' with its tail?

Yes, a cat uses its tail to send messages about how it is feeling. When a cat holds its tail straight up it is saying 'hello'. If it is sweeping its tail from side to side it may be about to pounce or attack.

Measure
Gently, see if you can measure how long your cat's tail is using a tape measure.

Kitten holding its tail up

How do cats keep their claws sharp?

Cats keep their claws sharp by scratching. A cat will scratch most things, including furniture, so it is a good idea to buy a scratching post. Scratching removes old protective covers, called sheaths, from the claws.

Scratching post

Sniff!
A cat's sense of smell is about 14 times better than a human's – but not as good as a dog's!

Do cats dream?

Experts think that cats do dream. When a cat is asleep its paws and whiskers twitch sometimes. Scientists think that this is a sign a cat is dreaming, but they are not sure what they may be dreaming about!

Why do cats love catnip?

Catnip is a type of plant and it makes cats feel very excited! Many cats behave differently when they come near catnip — they rub themselves on the plant, roll around in it, lick it or eat it. Lots of cat toys contain catnip.

Cat eating catnip

Think

Can you think of some poems, rhymes or stories that have cats in them?

HOW do cats hunt?

A cat creeps towards its prey very slowly. It moves quietly and crouches low to the ground to stay hidden. The cat gets as close as it can then makes a final speedy dash and pounces on its catch.

A cat hunting in the grass

Mouse

PUSS in boots!

In the story *Puss in Boots*, written by Charles Perrault in 1697, a cat brings gifts to a king so his owner, a poor man, could meet and marry the king's daughter.

which cat went to sea in a pea-green boat?

The cat in the poem 'The Owl and the Pussycat', by Edward Lear. The author loved cats and drew many pictures of them. In the poem, the cat goes to sea with an owl.

Quiz time

Do you remember what you have read about cats and kittens? Here are some questions to test your memory. The pictures will help you. If you get stuck, read the pages again.

1. How does a cat show it's angry?

page 41

2. Why do kittens play?

page 42

3. How long do cats sleep?

page 43

4. How do cats carry their kittens?

page 44

5. Are black cats witches' cats?

page 45

6. Can cats and dogs be friends?

page 46

7. Why do cats eat grass?

page 47

8. What do kittens drink?

page 48

9. Are cats good climbers?

page 49

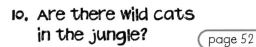

10. Are there wild cats in the jungle?

page 52

11. Are all cats furry?

page 61

12. How do cats keep their claws sharp?

page 63

13. Which cat went to sea in a pea-green boat?

page 65

Answers

1. It arches its back and makes its fur stand on end to make itself look bigger
2. Because it's fun, and it helps kittens to grow strong and to get on with other animals
3. About 16 hours a day
4. They carry their kittens in their mouths
5. No, but some people once believed they were
6. Yes, if they grow up together
7. It helps them to cough up fur from grooming
8. Their mother's milk
9. Yes, they are expert climbers
10. Wild cats, called jungle cats, live in forests in Asia
11. Most are, but the Sphynx cat is hairless
12. By scratching
13. The cat in the poem 'The Owl and the Pussycat'

Horses and ponies

Are horses the same as ponies?

Horses and ponies are in the same animal group, but ponies are smaller. The height of a horse or pony is measured in 'hands'. To be considered a pony, a horse must be less than 14.2 hands (148 centimetres) tall at the withers (base of the neck).

Horse

Food on the move!

Since the 1800s, nosebags have been used to feed horses on the move. They are also useful for horses that are messy eaters!

Farmer

Shire horses pulling a plough

which horses worked on farms?

Shire horses were bred to pull heavy farm carts and ploughs before modern tractors and trucks were invented. They were used for this job because they are big, heavy and strong.

calculate

Try working out your own height in hands. There are 10 centimetres (4 inches) in a hand.

 Pony

when were the first horse races?

People have probably raced horses since they first began taming them, over 5000 years ago. In ancient Greece, horse racing was part of the Olympic Games and the riders rode without saddles!

what are the points of a horse?

The points are the parts of a horse's body that you can see. Each point has a special name, such as withers, muzzle and fetlock. People who work with horses have to learn the names for all of the points.

Dock

Back

Hock

Fetlock

Hoof

count

How many socks and stockings can you find on the horses in this book?

Do horses have good eyesight?

Yes, they have excellent eyesight. They can see in almost every direction because their large eyes are on the sides of their head. This helps them to watch for predators (animals that hunt them).

Poll

Crest

Forelock

Withers

Muzzle

Magical horse!

A unicorn is a mythical horse with a horn on its head. Some people think the legend of unicorns came from the first sightings of rhinos!

Do horses and ponies wear socks?

No – but they have markings on their feet that are known as socks. A sock that goes up higher than the horse's knee is called a stocking. Horses can also have white marks on their faces, chests or heads.

Sock

Are horses and ponies colourful?

Yes they are! Horses and ponies have many different coat colours. Some of the colours and patterns have special names, such as bay (reddish-brown), chestnut (reddish-gold), dark bay (brown) and dun (sandy brown).

Chestnut
Reddish-gold

Skewbald
Patches of brown and white

Piebald
Patches of black and white

Palomino
Golden with white mane and tail

why do horses wear shoes?

Horses wear metal horseshoes to protect their feet, or hooves. If horses run on hard surfaces without shoes, their hooves can get worn down. People who fit horseshoes onto horses are called farriers.

Farrier

Draw

Draw a picture of a horse and colour it in. Choose a pattern, such as piebald, for its body.

How can you tell a horse's age?

Vets can tell how old a horse is by looking in its mouth. A horse's front teeth change shape as it ages – from oval to round, and then to triangular. Older horses' teeth also stick out more.

Dark bay
Brown

Old Billy!

Horses usually live to about 30 years old. But Old Billy, an English horse born in the 1700s, lived to be 62!

Grey
White to grey

Do horses understand people?

Horses are clever animals and they can learn to understand commands such as 'walk' and 'whoa' (stop). Riders can also give horses instructions by nudging or patting them. Most horses are friendly, and they like to be talked to and touched.

Horse

Owner

High-speed horses!

Horses are fast runners, even when carrying a rider. The fastest racehorses can reach speeds of more than 60 kilometres an hour.

RUN

Run 100 metres as fast as you can! Ask an adult to time how long it takes you.

what do horses like to eat?

Horses and ponies eat mainly grass, or hay (dried grass). They often eat throughout the day. Horses and ponies enjoy other foods such as oats, barley and apples.

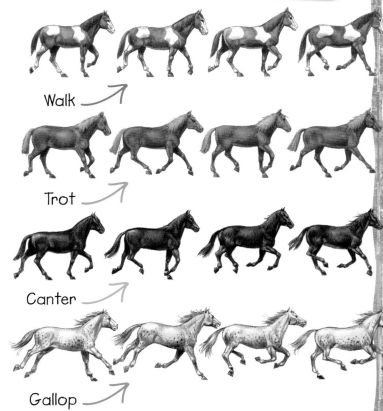

Walk

Trot

Canter

Gallop

How do horses gallop?

Horses can be trained to walk and run in four different ways — walk, trot, canter and gallop. When horses canter or gallop, there is a moment when all four feet are off the ground.

can horses swim well?

Swimming horse

Yes, horses are very good swimmers. They float well in water and swim by moving their legs in a paddling motion. Horse trainers sometimes take their horses swimming because it's good exercise and helps to build up their muscles.

Do some horses live in the wild?

Herds of wild horses live in many parts of the world. Most were originally tame horses that escaped from being kept by people. Only a few horses, such as the rare Przewalski's horse from Asia, are truly wild.

Cave horses!

There are ancient cave paintings of horses in the Lascaux cave in France. They were created over 17,000 years ago.

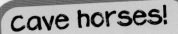

which horse was as small as a sheep?

Mesohippus was a prehistoric, sheep-sized horse that roamed the Earth around 35 million years ago. Like other early horses, it was much smaller than most horses and ponies today. It was about 60 centimetres tall.

Mesohippus

Swim

The next time you go swimming, try to paddle the same way that a horse swims.

which horses live in swamps?

Groups of beautiful, white Camargue horses live in marshy swamps in France. They are small, but strong and sure-footed. Camargues are ridden by bull herders and can also be used for competitions and trekking.

Camargues

Find out

Look in books and on the Internet to learn about other animals that live in swamps.

When do foals start to walk?

A newborn horse, called a foal, can walk just a few hours after birth. Being able to move around and find food helps them to survive, and escape from predators.

Foal

Handsome horses!

Knights used to dress their horses up for tournaments (knightly contests) and battles. The horses wore coloured coats called trappers and helmets called shaffrons.

Do horses like to be on their own?

Most horses prefer company. In the wild, they naturally live in groups, or herds. Tame horses are usually happiest if they are kept in stables or fields with other horses.

what is a hotblood?

Hotbloods are one of three types of horse. They came from the Middle East and Africa, and are often used in racing because they are fast. Coldblood horses are heavy, strong horses originally from colder areas in northern Europe. Warmbloods were bred by crossing hotbloods with coldbloods.

Warmblood

Hotblood

Coldblood

Why do horses wear plaits?

For shows and contests, a horse's owner may plait or decorate the long hair on its head and neck (mane). Plaiting helps the mane to stay neat as the horse moves around.

Black Beauty!

Black Beauty is a novel written by Anna Sewell in 1877, about a black horse. In the book, the horse (Black Beauty) tells the story of his life and the people he met.

Horse being groomed

Do horses need grooming?

Yes, horses need to be groomed to stay clean and healthy. A horse should be brushed all over, and its hooves should be cleaned out. This removes bugs that could cause diseases and it makes the horse's coat look glossy.

How does a rider control a horse?

A rider controls a horse using reins – straps attached to a bridle around the horse's face. By pulling gently on the reins, the rider can tell the horse which way to go. Riders also do this by nudging the horse with their knees.

Bridle

Rein

Bit

Make

Using empty egg cartons and boxes, make a cart for a toy horse to pull.

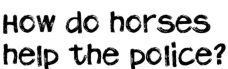

Handy horses!

Ancient artworks show that humans have been using horses to pull carts and carriages for about 5000 years.

How do horses help the police?

The police use horses for transport in places where vehicles can't go, such as on a festival site or at a crowded street protest. Riding up high, police officers can get a good view.

What are saddles for?

Saddles help riders stay safe and comfortable. A saddle is a leather seat that is strapped onto a horse's back by the girth. A rider's feet sit in the metal loops, called stirrups, attached to the saddle.

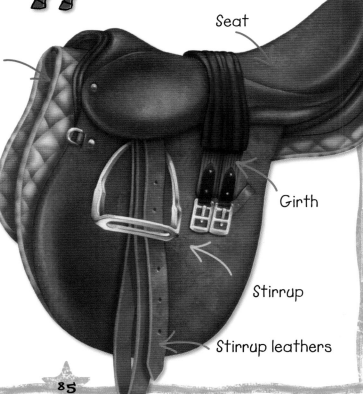

Seat

Padding

Girth

Stirrup

Stirrup leathers

Which pony is a champion jumper?

Rider

The **Connemara pony, which first came from Ireland, is great at jumping.** It can be ridden easily by adults and children. These ponies are often trained to take part in jumping and cross-country competitions, where horses have to jump over obstacles.

Jump

Set up some obstacles in your garden and see how high you can jump over them.

Did horses go to war?

Yes, horses have been ridden into battle since ancient times. They were trained to charge towards an enemy army without fear, and some wore special horse armour.

Warrior on horseback

Connemara pony

Horse of an emperor!

The Roman emperor Caligula was said to love his horse so much that he gave it its own house and servants!

What was chariot racing?

It was one of the most popular sports of the ancient Romans. In a race, horses pulled two-wheeled carts called chariots around a track called a 'circus'. There could be up to 12 chariots in each race.

Do horses have relatives?

Yes, they do. You can spot some of their relatives by their horse-like shape, such as zebras and donkeys. They belong to the same animal family as horses and ponies, called 'equids'. Horses are also cousins of rhinos and tapirs.

Zebras

Shetland ponies

Why are Shetland ponies so tough?

Shetland ponies come from the Shetland Islands, in the far north of Scotland, where it is often very cold and windy. They have developed short, stocky bodies and thick coats to keep warm.

How do horses talk to each other?

Horses use noises and touch to communicate. For example, 'whinnying' to call to each other, squealing or snorting to show alarm or excitement and nuzzling to greet and comfort each other.

what does an angry horse look like?

If a horse or pony is angry or unhappy, it flattens its ears backwards against its head. It may also show the whites of its eyes by opening them wide. If you see a horse doing this, you should stay away in case it bites or kicks.

Ears are back

Think

Think about how you can tell when a person is angry or happy. How do they show it?

what makes horses and ponies ill?

Eating poisonous plants. Horses and ponies can't be sick, so if they eat something that's bad for them, they can't bring it back up. Foxgloves, acorns, laburnum and ragwort are some of the plants that horses and ponies should not eat.

No stirrups!

The ancient Greeks rode horses, but they didn't have stirrups to put their feet into. This meant that they often fell off!

Acorns

Foxglove

Laburnum

Ragwort

Do horses drink a lot of water?

Yes — horses should always have a water supply. They need plenty of water to help wash down their food, otherwise they can get stomach pain called colic. However, some horses don't like water, especially if it's too cold.

where are horses kept?

Horses are kept in special buildings called stables. Each horse has its own room or stall, with straw or sawdust on the floor. The stalls have to be cleaned, or 'mucked out', every day to remove the horse's manure (droppings).

Owner 'mucking out'

Mother and foal

Straw

Carrots

DO cowboys ride horses?

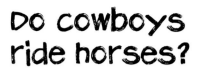

Yes — cowboys traditionally rode on horseback to move cows around their ranches (large American farms). Many cowboys still ride horses, but they also ride bulls at rodeos.

Friends or enemies?

Cowboys and 'Indians' (Native Americans) were often shown fighting in old films. In real life, this rarely happened.

what is a rodeo?

A rodeo is a show or contest where cowboys and cowgirls display their skills. These include riding wild horses, rounding up cows or using a lasso (loop of rope) Rodeos are popular in the United States, South America and Australia.

Discover

Look in books or on the Internet to find out what clothes cowboys wear.

Lasso

Cowboy

Cow

can horses dance?

Some horses can be trained to perform special ballet-like movements known as dressage. The moves include skipping, prancing, dancing sideways, balancing in difficult positions, hopping on their back legs and leaping high into the air. Austria's Lipizzaner horses are famous for their amazing dressage shows.

Lipizzaner horse

What is the smallest horse?

The Falabella miniature horse is the smallest. It is around 8 hands (80 centimetres) tall — as small as some breeds of dog! They are friendly and clever, but too small for most people to ride.

Falabella

Dance

What are your best dance moves? Try leaping high into the air like a Lipizzaner horse.

Do horses fight each other?

Yes, in the wild. A herd of wild horses has just one adult male, called a stallion. When one stallion challenges another, they rear up and fight with their front hooves.

Mini riders!

Jockeys who ride racehorses have to be as small and light as possible to make racing easier for the horse.

Quiz time

Do you remember what you have read about horses and ponies? Here are some questions to test your memory. The pictures will help you. If you get stuck, read the pages again.

3. Which horse was as small as a sheep?

page 79

4. Which horses live in swamps?

page 80

1. Which horses worked on farms?

page 71

5. What is a hotblood?

page 82

2. How can you tell a horse's age?

page 75

6. Do horses need grooming?

page 83

7. What are saddles for?

page 85

11. Do cowboys ride horses?

page 93

page 95

8. Did horses go to war?

page 87

12. What is the smallest horse?

13. Do horses fight each other?

page 95

9. Why are Shetland ponies so tough?

page 89

10. Do horses drink a lot of water?

page 91

Answers

1. Shire horses
2. Experts can tell a horse's age by looking at its teeth
3. A prehistoric, sheep-sized horse called *Mesohippus*
4. Camargue horses
5. A type of horse that is fast, slender and often used in racing
6. Yes, to keep them clean and healthy
7. A saddle is a leather seat placed on a horse's back to keep its rider safe and comfortable
8. Yes, horses have been ridden into war since ancient times
9. Because the weather on the Shetland Islands, where they live, is often very cold and windy
10. Yes
11. Yes – cowboys traditionally ride horses
12. The Falabella miniature horse
13. Yes, some wild horses do

97

Baby animals

which animal is the best mum?

Many animals take great care of their young, but the orang-utan is one of the most caring. They feed their babies for at least three years and cuddle up close every night. A young orang-utan stays with its mum until it is about seven or eight years old.

Baby orang-utan

Big eater!

A baby blue whale drinks nearly 400 litres of its mother's milk every day. That's about five bathfuls!

which frog is the best dad?

The green poison-dart frog is! The male guards his eggs while they develop. Then, after the eggs have hatched into tadpoles, he takes them to a safe pool of water to grow.

Tadpoles

Find

What did you look like as a baby? Find some photos of you when you were a few months old.

Green poison-dart frog

what do baby frogs look like?

Baby frogs, called tadpoles, look very different from their parents. They are little swimming creatures with a tail and no legs. They have gills for breathing in water. As they get bigger, tadpoles grow legs and lose their tail.

Why do fawns have spots?

The spotty coat of a fawn (baby deer) makes it hard to see in its forest home. This is because the sun shines through leaves and twigs, making light spots on the forest floor — just like the spots on the fawn's coat.

Imagine
Pretend you are a mother bird and make a soft nest using blankets and pillows.

Fawn

102

How do monkeys clean their babies?

Monkeys groom their young with their fingers and pick out bits of dead skin, insects and dirt. Many animals also lick their babies to keep them clean.

Macaque monkey family

Trunk call

Elephants use their trunks for many things, such as grabbing food from trees. Baby elephants have to learn to control their trunks.

What do baby sharks eat?

Some eat other baby sharks! The eggs of the sand tiger shark hatch inside the mother's body. The first young to hatch then feed on the other eggs. When the sharks are born they are about one metre long.

Why do kangaroos have pouches?

Kangaroos have pouches to keep their babies safe. A baby kangaroo is called a joey and it is very weak and tiny when it is born. It lives in its mum's pouch where it feeds and grows until it is strong enough to look after itself.

Joey

Think

Puppy, kitten, chick... how many other names for baby animals can you think of?

Are turtles born in the sea?

Turtles live in the sea but lay their eggs on land. The mother turtle crawls up onto the beach and digs a pit in which to lay her eggs. When the eggs hatch, the babies make their way down to the sea.

Baby loggerhead turtle

Which animal has the longest pregnancy?

Pregnancy is the word used for the time it takes for a baby to grow inside its mother. The female elephant has the longest pregnancy of any animal — up to 21 months — that's nearly two years!

Watch out!

Family life is dangerous for the praying mantis, a type of insect. The mum is bigger than the dad — and she often eats him!

Why do baby animals play?

Lots of baby animals, such as otters pups, love to play. It helps them grow stronger and learn skills they will need as adults. Play fighting and chasing helps young animals learn how to hunt and catch prey.

Otter pups

which bird makes the biggest nest?

The bald eagle makes the biggest nest of any bird. The largest ever seen was about 6 metres deep — big enough for a giraffe to hide in! The eagles use the same nest every year and add more sticks to it each time.

Bald eagle in its nest

Biggest egg

The ostrich lays the biggest egg of any bird. It weighs more than 1.5 kg — that's the same as 24 hen's eggs!

Are baby snakes dangerous?

Some are, yes. Not all types of snake use venom to kill their prey, but those that do, such as rattlesnakes, can give a deadly bite soon after they are born.

ASK
Find out how much you weighed at birth and measure out the same amount using weighing scales.

where do baby rabbits live?

Baby rabbits are called kits and they live in a cosy nest called a warren. The warren is underground and lined with hay, straw and fur to help keep the kits warm.

Warren

Kits

Do foals stay close to their mums?

Yes they do – foals stay close to their mums for safety. They are able to walk soon after birth, as in the wild they may have to move quickly to escape from animals that hunt them.

Foal

Greedy!

Caterpillars spend all their time eating and can grow to more than 30,000 times the size they were when they hatched!

Draw

What does your favourite baby animal look like? Once you have decided, draw a picture.

Do baby animals laugh?

Some do! Gorillas, chimps and orang-utans laugh when they're playing or tickling each other, just like we do. Scientists think that some other animals, such as dogs, may also laugh.

How do polar bear cubs keep warm?

Polar bear cubs

Polar bears live in the Arctic, where it is always very cold. The mother bear digs a den under the snow where her cubs are born. They live there until they are three months old. It is surprisingly warm and cosy in the den!

PLAY

Would you be a good mum or dad? Pretend your teddy bear is a baby and look after it carefully all day.

① Caterpillar hatches from its egg

② Pupa is formed

③ Butterfly breaks out of its pupa

when do caterpillars become butterflies?

When a caterpillar has grown as big as it can, it stops eating and makes a hard case around itself called a pupa. Inside the pupa the caterpillar's body changes into a butterfly. The butterfly then breaks out of the pupa and flies away.

④ Butterfly flies away

Big baby

Blue whales have the world's biggest babies. They are about 8 metres long at birth – that's roughly as long as two cars!

why do scorpions carry their young?

Scorpions carry their babies on their backs until they are big and strong enough to take care of themselves. They climb onto their mum's back when they hatch and are carried around for the first two weeks.

when can squirrels leave their nests?

Baby squirrels are born tiny and helpless with very little fur. They stay in their tree trunk nest for seven to ten weeks, feeding and growing. By ten weeks they are nearly fully grown and can look after themselves.

Mother and baby squirrels

112

why do spiders leave home?

Baby spiders are called spiderlings, and as they grow they need to move to new areas to find food. Each spider spins silken threads from the tip of its body. These catch the air like kites and carry the spider to a new home.

Think

Try to think of as many different animals that make nests and draw pictures of them.

Tall tales

Giraffes are the tallest of all animals. Even a newborn giraffe is around 1.8 metres tall – that's as big as a grown-up person!

Shark egg

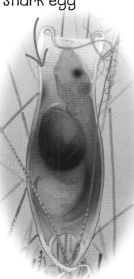

Do sharks lay eggs?

Some sharks do. Each egg grows in a strong case, sometimes called a mermaid's purse. The case has long threads that attach to seaweed or rocks to help keep it safe.

Egg case

Shark pup

Do sloths give birth upside down?

Yes, they do! Sloths give birth to their babies hanging upside down from trees! The baby then stays close to its mother, clinging to her fur for the first nine months of its life.

Sloth mother and baby

Make

Use some play dough to make a bird's nest and then make some little eggs to place inside.

How do penguin chicks keep warm?

Penguins usually live in cold places and keep warm by huddling together — the chicks stand on their parents feet. The penguins keep swapping places so each gets a turn at being in the middle — the warmest spot.

Queen bee

A queen honeybee lays all the eggs for her hive but she doesn't look after them, The worker bees take care of the babies for her!

Mother bird and chick

How do baby birds get food?

Most baby birds are fed by their parents. Adult birds work very hard to find tasty morsels to bring back to their chicks. The babies always seem to be hungry and wait with their beaks wide open.

Do baby elephants leave their herd?

Only male elephants ever leave their close family groups, called herds. Young elephants stay with their mums for many years. The males will eventually leave and live alone or with other males, but females stay with their herd.

Elephant mother

Calf

make

Find lots of pictures of baby animals. Stick them on a big sheet of paper to make a poster.

How does a chick get out of its egg?

A baby bird has a tiny spike, called an egg tooth, on its beak. When it is ready to hatch, the chick makes a little hole in the shell with the egg tooth and then struggles out.

Chick breaking out

Egg

Busy mum

Virginia opossums can have up to 13 babies at a time. The babies are tiny at birth and stay with their mum for about three months.

Do badgers keep their nests clean?

Yes they do. Badgers live in underground nests called setts, and use grass, leaves and straw for bedding. The badgers bring their bedding out of the sett to air it and then throw out old, dirty bedding.

Why do lion cubs play fight?

To practise the hunting skills they have learnt from their mothers. Female lions train their cubs to hunt by bringing small animals for the cubs to catch. Then the young lions go and watch their mothers hunting from a safe distance.

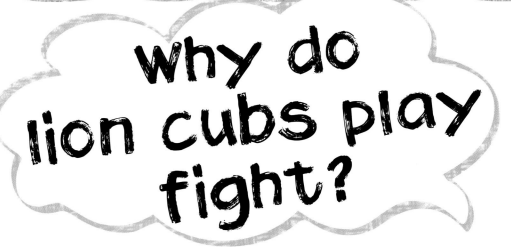

Lion cubs play fighting

① Baby snake breaking eggshell

② Fully hatched

Do snakes lay eggs?

Most snakes do lay eggs, although some give birth to live babies. A snake's eggshell is tough, bendy and almost watertight, unlike a hen's egg. Female snakes usually lay about five to 20 eggs at a time.

Big mouth

The mouth brooder fish keeps its eggs safe in its mouth while they develop and grow.

Why are some eggs pear-shaped?

A guillemot is a type of sea bird that nests on cliffs. Its eggs are pear-shaped with one end more pointed than the other. This shape means that the egg rolls round in a circle if knocked, and won't roll off the cliff.

Paint

Ask an adult to hard-boil some eggs for you. Then paint pictures on the shells.

when do fox cubs leave their dens?

Fox cubs are born blind and helpless so they stay in their dens for the first few weeks. If their home is disturbed, the mother fox may move her cubs to a new den. Most cubs make their first outing when they are four weeks old.

Fox cubs

why do cuckoos lay eggs quickly?

Because they lay their eggs in other birds' nests, instead of making their own. The other bird then looks after and feeds the cuckoo chick. A cuckoo lays an egg in just nine seconds – most birds take several minutes!

clever baby

A gorilla baby develops more quickly than a human baby. They can crawl at about two months and walk at nine months.

Think

When human babies want their parents they cry. What noise do you think a baby bird makes to get attention?

which bird has the safest nest?

The female hornbill makes her nest in a tree hole. The male then blocks up the hole with mud so that she and the eggs are safe from hunters. He leaves a hole for her beak so he can feed her while she's inside.

Male hornbill feeding female

when can cheetah cubs live alone?

Cheetah cubs can live alone when they are about 18 months old. Before they are ready to leave their mother they must learn to catch their own food. They learn how to hunt by watching their mother.

Cheetah cubs

Why are harp seal pups white?

Harp seals live in the snowy Arctic. The pups have white coats to keep them hidden from polar bears, which hunt them. Their fluffy coats also help to keep the seal pups warm.

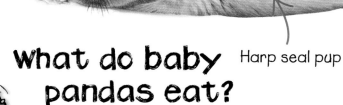

Harp seal pup

What do baby pandas eat?

A baby panda drinks its mother's milk until it is about nine months old. Adult pandas feed on bamboo, and the baby starts to eat this when it is about six months old.

Discover

Some baby wasps feed on dung – animal poo! Find out what some other baby animals like to eat.

Marvellous mum

An octopus is a great mum. She guards her eggs for about a month while they grow, and she doesn't even leave them to find food.

can rhino mums be fierce?

Yes they can – a rhino mum can be fierce when she's looking after her young. If hyaenas or other animals try to attack her baby, she charges towards them with her sharp horn to scare them away.

Rhino mum and calf

Are baby hedgehogs born prickly?

Luckily for hedgehog mums, their babies' have very soft spines at first. They harden as the baby grows until they are extremely sharp and strong.

Find out

Ask your parents how old you were when you could first crawl, walk and talk.

Are alligators good parents?

Alligator dads do nothing for their babies, but an alligator mum is a caring parent. She guards her eggs and helps the young to hatch. The mum may then gently lift the tiny babies in her mouth and carry them to water.

Keep warm

The Australian mallee fowl lays its eggs in a mound of earth and leaves. The bird checks the temperature with its beak to make sure its eggs stay warm.

Baby alligator

Quiz time

Do you remember what you have read about baby animals? Here are some questions to test your memory. The pictures will help you. If you get stuck, read the pages again.

3. Are baby snakes dangerous?

page 107

4. Do foals stay close to their mums?

page 109

1. Why do fawns have spots?

page 102

5. Why do scorpions carry their young?

page 111

2. Are turtles born in the sea?

page 105

6. Do sharks lay eggs?

page 113

page 114

7. Do sloths give birth upside down?

page 121

11. Which bird has the safest nest?

12. Why are harp seal pups white?

page 123

8. How does a chick get out of its egg?

page 117

9. Do badgers keep their nests clean?

page 117

13. Can rhino mums be fierce?

page 124

10. Do snakes lay eggs?

page 119

Answers

1. To help them blend in with their forest homes
2. No, they are born on land
3. The types that have poison are, yes
4. A few hours after birth
5. To protect them from harm
6. Yes, some do
7. Yes
8. Using their egg tooth to make a hole in the shell, then struggle out
9. Yes
10. Most do, yes
11. The hornbill
12. To make them hard to spot in the snow
13. Yes they can – they charge at predators

penguins

what is a penguin?

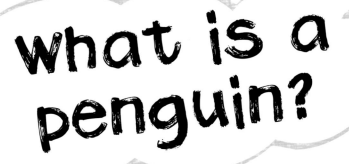

A penguin is a bird that spends most of its life in the ocean. It only comes onto land to lay eggs, look after its chicks and grow new feathers. Although penguins cannot fly, they are brilliant at swimming and diving.

Humboldt penguin

Are penguins the only flightless birds?

No, but most other flightless birds, such as ostriches and emus, live on land. They can run very fast to escape from enemies. The flightless cormorants of the Galapagos Islands are the only other seabirds that cannot fly.

Why can't penguins fly?

Penguins' wings are too short and stiff for flying. They are called flippers, and are a good size and shape for pushing the penguin along underwater. Penguins 'fly' underwater at about 8 kilometres an hour.

Royal penguin

Pretend
Can you move like a penguin? Hold your arms straight out at your sides and flap them up and down like flippers.

Is there only one kind of penguin?

No – there are 17 different species (kinds). They are mostly black and white, but the little penguin is blue and white. Some have black bands on their chests and heads. Others have bright crests or ear patches.

Magellanic penguin

Fjordland penguin

King penguin

Think

Look at the pictures of penguins in this book. Choose your favourite and make up your own name for it.

Do penguins like pasta?

No, but one type of penguin was named after the group of men who introduced macaroni pasta to England. The men wore feathers in their hats – a bit like the macaroni penguin's crest feathers.

Sports star!

Penguins don't need skis to get around in snow. They use their strong flippers to pull themselves uphill. To go downhill, they lie on their tummies and slide, like toboggans.

How big are penguins?

Different types of penguin are different sizes. The emperor penguin is the biggest and the little or fairy penguin is the smallest. The emperor is more than 20 times heavier than the little penguin, which weighs no more than a bag of sugar!

Little penguin is up to 45 centimetres tall

Emperor penguin is up to 1.15 metres tall

which penguin wears a helmet?

The chinstrap penguin does! It has a band of black feathers that run from ear to ear under its bill. This makes it look as if it is wearing a helmet, with a strap under its chin.

Chinstrap penguin

scary penguins!

An Adélie penguin will stare and point at rivals to keep them away from its nesting area. It may even beat other penguins with its flippers!

when is a penguin like a donkey?

When it's a jackass penguin! This penguin makes loud braying calls, which sound similar to the noises made by donkeys. Jackass penguins are also called African penguins because they live around the coasts of southern Africa.

Snares penguin

why do some penguins have yellow hair?

Crested penguins have long yellow feathers above their eyes. This makes them look as if they have spiky yellow hair! Their colourful head crests help these penguins to recognize their friends and relatives and attract mates.

Are penguins tidy?

Adélie penguin

No – penguin nests are noisy, busy, messy places. But one group of penguins does have long tail feathers that sweep the ground as they walk. They are called brush-tailed penguins and include chinstrap penguins, Adélie penguins and gentoo penguins.

Shark surprise!

Like penguins, sharks are a dark colour on top and a light colour underneath. This helps them to sneak up on their prey in surprise attacks!

why are most penguins black and white?

A penguin's colours help to camouflage (disguise) it from predators and prey. From above, its black back blends with the dark water below. From below, its white tummy blends with the light of the sky.

King penguin chick still with fluffy feathers

Do penguins mind getting wet?

Only when they are young. Penguin chicks have fluffy feathers at first, which are warm, but not waterproof. Chicks cannot go into the water until they have grown all their waterproof adult feathers.

King penguin chick growing waterproof feathers

Do polar bears live with penguins?

No – they never even meet! Penguins live in the southern half of the world and polar bears live in the north. Many kinds of penguins live in or around freezing Antarctica, but a few live in warmer places, such as Africa or New Zealand.

Adélie penguins

Do penguins get sunburnt?

Galapagos penguins live on the hot Galapagos Islands. Swimming in the ocean helps them to keep cool. On land, they hold their flippers over their feet to stop them getting sunburnt!

Penguin on ice!

Penguins have webbed feet with strong claws to stop them sliding on slippery ice. They hold their flippers out to help them balance when they waddle across ice and snow.

Discover

Look through this book and find one penguin that lives in a hot place and one penguin that lives in a cold place.

Jackass penguins

How do penguins keep cool?

Penguins that live in warmer places lose heat from patches of bare skin on their head, flippers and feet. They can also move into the shade or shelter in underground burrows to escape the hottest hours of day.

Why are penguins good swimmers?

Penguins have a smooth shape, so they move smoothly underwater. Their heavy bones help them to dive deep, and their long, flat flippers give power to their swimming strokes. Penguins use their tails and feet to steer and brake.

King penguins

Do leopards eat penguins?

No – but a spotted seal called a leopard seal does. These fast-swimming hunters have wide mouths and sharp teeth. They sneak up on penguins, carry them to the surface, and swallow them.

Leopard seal

Gentoo penguin

Sleepy penguins!

Penguins snooze at almost any time and can even take short naps while swimming! They mostly sleep at night and can fall asleep when they are standing or lying down.

Float

When you next go swimming, try floating. Take a deep breath, lie back and hold your arms and legs out in a star shape.

Can penguins hold their breath?

Yes, they hold their breath when they dive. Emperors can hold their breath for up to 18 minutes because they can store lots of oxygen inside their bodies. Little penguins can only hold their breath for about a minute.

Which penguin can tap-dance?

Mumble the emperor penguin, in the movie *Happy Feet* can! In a world where every penguin needs a special song to attract a soulmate, poor Mumble has a terrible singing voice. Instead he has to tap-dance his way into the heart of the penguin he loves.

Mumble the tap-dancing penguin

Think

Make up a story about a penguin who wants to star in a musical. Does his or her dream come true?

why do penguins go on long journeys?

Penguins nest on land but have to make long journeys back to the sea to collect food for their chicks. Parent Adélie penguins may travel up to 120 kilometres in search of food.

Bounce, bounce!

A penguin's layers of fat cushion its body from bumps when it moves over rocks. Its strong, leathery skin gives extra protection.

Rockhopper penguins →

HOW fast can penguins walk?

Penguins can walk as fast as people. They look clumsy on land, but they can leap high out of the water onto ice and use their sharp claws and strong bills to pull themselves up rocks. Rockhopper penguins jump from rock to rock, which is how they got their name.

what do penguins eat?

Penguins are meat-eaters and catch their food in the sea. They eat mainly fish, squid and shrimp-like krill. Smaller penguins eat a lot of krill, which float on the surface of the sea at night. Larger penguins dive deeper and feed mainly on squid.

Big meal!

A penguin has no teeth, so it swallows its food whole. A sharp bill and spines on its tongue help the penguin to grip slippery, wriggly fish.

Humboldt penguin catching a fish

HOW do penguins feed their chicks?

Penguins cough up food to feed to their chicks. Parent birds hunt in the sea, storing food in their stomachs or in special pouches in their throats. Then they carry the food back to their hungry chicks.

Chinstrap penguin

Chicks

Can penguins catch food in the dark?

Some penguins catch their food deep down in the ocean where it is very dark. They have excellent eyesight and may also use their other senses, such as smell and hearing, to find food.

count

See how many times you eat fish in a month. Fish is very good for you, especially oily fish such as sardines and tuna.

Are penguins show-offs?

Male penguins show off to impress females. They stretch up tall, point their bills towards the sky, beat their flippers and call loudly. Male chinstrap penguins put on a very noisy show — they sound like donkeys or hissing cats!

Chinstrap penguin displaying

How long can emperors go without food?

While keeping his egg warm, a male emperor penguin doesn't eat for more than 15 weeks. By the time his mate returns from her feeding trip out at sea, he may have lost up to half of his body weight.

Female

Male gentoo
with pebble

Build

Collect some pebbles from the beach, or some stones from the garden and build a stone nest for one of your toy animals.

when do penguins give presents?

When they are building a nest of pebbles, male Gentoo and Adélie penguins sometimes give their mates pebbles as presents. This helps make the nest bigger and shows that the males are serious about bringing up a family.

Take a bow!

A pair of Adélie penguins bow to each other when they meet. They also stretch upwards with bills open, calling loudly and swaying from side to side.

Why do penguins nest together?

So they can huddle together for warmth, and so there are plenty of eyes to keep watch for predators. In many of the places where penguins live, there is little space for nesting. A group of nesting penguins is called a rookery.

Gentoo penguin rookery

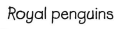
Royal penguins

when do penguins fight?

Penguins are irritable birds, often squabbling over nesting spaces and even stealing pebbles or other nesting materials from each other. They fight with their sharp beaks and strong flippers. Some fights are so fierce that eggs are crushed.

Discover

Find out how many penguins live together in a rookery. What is the biggest number you can discover?

Fantastic fisherman!

Penguins are among only a few fish-eating animals that can survive in the freezing oceans around Antarctica. This means there is plenty of food for them to collect for their chicks!

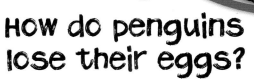

How do penguins lose their eggs?

In hot weather, jackass penguins sometimes have to leave their nests to cool down in the sea. By the time they return, their eggs may have been eaten or stolen by seabirds.

where do emperors keep their eggs?

When a female emperor penguin lays her egg, her mate puts it on top of his feet. He keeps it warm under a flap of skin — rather like a tea cosy. If the egg falls onto the ice, it will freeze and the chick inside will die.

Emperor penguins

Do penguins lay lots of eggs?

Emperor and king penguins only lay one egg but most other types of penguin lay two. The first chick to hatch often receives the most food, so it is more likely to survive than the second chick.

Hungry chicks!

Penguin chicks may be tiny when they hatch, but they grow fast and are always hungry! Parent birds are kept busy finding enough food for them to eat.

Emperor penguin

How do penguins find their chicks?

Penguin parents can pick out the high-pitched calls of their own chicks amongst the noise of a busy rookery. Young chicks stretch up and beg for food, while older chicks peck at their parents' bills to make them cough up food.

Chicks

which enemies eat eggs and chicks?

Hungry seabirds, such as gulls and skuas, lurk around the edge of penguin rookeries. They are always ready to take an easy meal of a penguin egg or chick. Parent penguins defend their eggs and chicks fiercely, and will not give them up without a fight.

King penguin

Skua

Egg

Draw

Sketch a picture of young penguins at a nursery school learning their letters, numbers and colours.

Do penguins go to school?

No, but their parents leave them in groups called nurseries. This happens when they are about seven weeks old. The chicks huddle together for warmth while their parents go off to sea to collect food for them.

Nursery of emperor chicks

Beware of the dog?

Dogs, cats, foxes and ferrets kill the chicks of yellow-eyed penguins. This species lives in New Zealand and is becoming rare.

Would a penguin peck a person?

Yes it would! Penguins are fierce birds and will attack people if they feel threatened. Thick jackets help to protect people from penguin bites.

quiz time

Do you remember what you have read about penguins? Here are some questions to test your memory. The pictures will help you. If you get stuck, read the pages again.

3. Which penguin wears a helmet?
   page 134

4. Why are most penguins black and white?
   page 137

5. Do polar bears live with penguins?
   page 138

1. Why can't penguins fly?
   page 131

6. Do leopards eat penguins?
   page 141

2. Do penguins like pasta?
   page 133

7. Why do penguins go on long journeys?

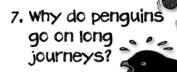

page 143

8. How do penguins feed their chicks?

page 145

9. How long can emperors go without food?

page 146

10. Why do penguins nest together?

page 148

11. How do penguins find their chicks?

page 151

12. Would a penguin peck a person?

page 153

13. Are penguins in trouble?

page 155

Answers

1. Because their wings are too short and stiff for flying
2. No, but there is a type of penguin called the macaroni penguin
3. The chinstrap penguin's feathers make it look like it is wearing a helmet
4. To camouflage them from predators and prey
5. No – they never even meet
6. No, but leopard seals do
7. To collect food for their chicks
8. They store food in their throats or stomachs and cough it up for their chicks
9. More than 15 weeks
10. For warmth, and so there are lots of them to keep watch for predators
11. By listening for their high-pitched calls
12. Yes!
13. Yes – they are suffering from lack of food, pollution, being hit by boats, and the destruction of their nesting sites

Bears

what is a bear?

A bear is a mammal. Mammals have warm blood, fur or hair, and they feed their babies on milk. Bears have big heads, short legs and thick fur. Female bears give birth to two or three babies (cubs) at a time.

Bear president!

Teddy bears are named after an American president called Teddy Roosevelt. He once refused to shoot a bear. After this, toy bears were called teddies.

Brown bear

Cubs

where do bears live?

Spectacled bears live only in the mountains of South America. Each type of bear has its own favourite place to live, from the icy north to hot rainforests.

Spectacled bear

Pretend
Imagine you are a bear and see how fast you can run on all fours, then race your friends.

How fast are bears?

Bears usually move slowly on all fours, but they can run surprisingly fast when they have to. Brown bears can charge at 50 kilometres an hour — much faster than most people!

Are all bears the same?

No – there are eight different kinds of bear! Each kind has different colours and markings. The easiest bears to recognize are the black-and-white giant panda and the white polar bear.

Giant panda

American black bear

Sun bear

Moon bear

Polar bear

Brown bear

Sloth bear

Spectacled bear

when is a panda red?

When it's a red panda! Red pandas are not actually bears. They belong to the raccoon family. When it's cold, red pandas curl their long, furry tails around their bodies to keep warm.

Red panda

It's all in the name!

Some ancient peoples thought it would anger bear spirits to call a bear by its name. They made up different names instead, such as 'Darling Old One' or 'Owner of the Earth'.

which bear is not a bear?

A koala bear! Even though koalas are sometimes called 'koala bears', they are not related to bears. Koalas have pouches. They live in Australia and eat eucalyptus leaves.

Find

Ask your friends what names they have given their teddies. How many different names can you find?

which bears are the biggest?

The biggest bears are the brown bears of Kodiak Island in Alaska, and polar bears. Both of these giant bears can weigh as much as a small car! The Kodiak bear has bigger bones than other types of brown bear.

Kodiak bear

Did people live with giant bears?

Yes – people hunted giant cave bears during the last Ice Age. They carved ornaments from their bones. These giant bears died out about 11,500 years ago.

Tallest bear!

The polar bear is the tallest bear alive today. The biggest one measured so far was 3.6 metres tall – that's twice the height of a tall person!

Draw

Create a height chart for your toy animals. Measure each one and draw lines on the chart.

Brown bear

can bears walk like us?

Yes they can! Bears rear up on two legs to get a good view of what is around them or to scare away enemies. Spectacled bear mothers can even walk along on two legs when they are holding their cubs.

Are bears good at climbing trees?

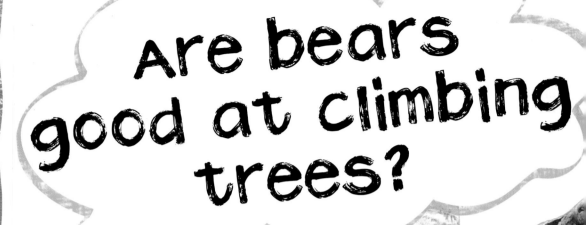

American black bear cubs

Yes! Bears have strong muscles in their legs and shoulders, which help them to scramble up tree trunks easily. Their long, curved claws give a firm grip on tree trunks and branches.

How long are a bear's claws?

Sun bear's paw and claws

A bear's thick, sharp claws are longer than your fingers! Unlike cats, bears can't pull their claws back into their paws. Bears use their claws for climbing trees, finding food and digging holes (dens) for sleeping or resting.

Poor panda!

Pandas sometimes fall out of trees. Their thick fur helps to cushion their bodies as they land.

Do bears build nests?

Bears don't usually build nests, but moon bears build leafy platforms in trees and sleep there. Spectacled bears also build nests in trees from the branches.

Pretend

Imagine you are a moon bear and build a cosy nest of leaves or cushions.

Do pandas ever stop eating?

Giant panda

Not very often! Giant pandas eat mainly bamboo, which is a type of tall, woody grass. Bamboo does not contain much goodness, so pandas have to spend most of their time eating to get the nutrients they need.

why do bears go fishing?

Bears find it easy to catch salmon when these big fish swim up rivers. Some bears fish from the riverbanks, but others wade right into the water and scoop up fish with their huge paws.

Grizzly bears

Seal supper!

Polar bears wait beside a seal's breathing hole in the ice. When the seal swims up to the hole for air, one swipe from the bear's giant paw kills the seal straight away.

Swim

When you next go swimming, try jumping out of the water like a salmon and see if someone can catch you!

which bear has the longest tongue?

The sun bear has the longest tongue — it is up to 25 centimetres long! This is very useful for licking up small bugs and reaching into cracks in trees.

Are sloth bears noisy?

Yes! When sloth bears feed at a termite mound, the noise they make can be heard up to 100 metres away! The bears make a tube with their lips and tongue and suck up lots of the tiny termites very quickly.

Sloth bears

Spectacled bear

Make

Draw a bear face on a paper plate. Cut holes for the eyes and use string to tie your mask on.

HOW good is a bear's sense of smell?

Bears have long noses and an excellent sense of smell. A bear often lifts its head to sniff the air, picking up smelly messages about food, danger or other bears.

Football bear!

Some sports teams, such as the Chicago Bears, are named after bears because they are strong, powerful animals.

Do bears have good eyesight?

Bears have small eyes and rely on their senses of smell and hearing more than their sense of sight. Their eyesight is about the same as a person with good eyesight. Bears can see in colour, which helps them to find fruits and berries.

which bear is a good swimmer?

Polar bears are strong swimmers.
Mothers teach their cubs to swim while
they are small. These bears use their
huge front paws to paddle through the
water and their back legs
for steering.

Polar bear

Cub

How did moon bears get their name?

Moon bears are named after the white or cream patch of fur on their chests, which is shaped like a crescent moon. These bears live in Asia and are also called Asiatic black bears.

Moon bear

Home alone!

Bears live alone, but they may gather in groups to feed. A group of bears is called a sloth, because people thought bears were slow and lazy, like sloths.

Think

Look at the bears in this book and make up some different names for a group of bears.

Do bears have picnics?

Teddy bears might do, but real bears don't. They eat whatever food is available at different times of year. Most bears eat a wide range of food, from grass, berries and honey to insects, fish, birds and mammals.

where do bears go in winter?

Bears that live in places with cold winters sleep through the winter, because there is little food for them to eat. They sleep inside a den, which may be a hole dug in the ground or a safe, sheltered place such as a cave.

Brown bear

which bear builds a snow cave?

Female polar bears build a snow cave and give birth to their tiny cubs in the middle of winter. The mother bear doesn't eat or drink until the cubs are big and strong enough to leave the den, up to five or six months later.

Polar bear

count

How many hours do you sleep each night? Work out how many hours you sleep in a week.

why do bears feast in autumn?

There is lots of food for bears to eat in autumn, such as berries, nuts, fish and insects. Bears eat as much as they can and become quite fat.

shrinking bear!

During their winter sleep bears don't eat. They use up the energy stored in their body as fat. Bears may lose up to half their body weight by the end of the winter.

when do cubs open their eyes?

Bear cubs are born with their eyes shut. They don't open their eyes until they are about six weeks old. Spectacled bears have pale fur around their eyes, which makes them look like they are wearing glasses!

story bears!

Bears are included in many famous stories, such as *Goldilocks and the Three Bears*.

Spectacled bear cubs

Do father bears look after their cubs?

American black bear

Cubs

No – mother bears bring up the cubs. The cubs drink their mother's milk. She teaches them how to find food and shelter, and how to escape from danger.

How big are bear cubs?

Bear cubs are very small. Polar bear cubs are no bigger than guinea pigs when they are born!

Discover
Use the Internet to find out how much a giant panda cub weighs when it is born.

Do bears give piggybacks?

Cubs

Sloth bear mothers do! The cubs ride around on her back until they are about nine months old. She has a special patch of fur for the cubs to hang on to. These piggyback rides keep them safe from enemies, including other bears.

Sloth bear

why do male bears fight?

Male bears fight over food, female bears and places to live. They have sharp teeth and claws, and can give each other serious injuries. Most of the time bears keep away from each other to avoid fights.

Brown bears

No winners!

Bears sometimes fight Siberian tigers. They are both strong and the same size, so it is difficult for either to win!

which bears fought for the romans?

Atlas bears were captured by the Romans and made to fight people called gladiators. These fierce fights were arranged to entertain people, but were very cruel to the bears.

Draw

Look at pictures of Roman soldiers in books and draw your teddy bear wearing armour.

which bear loves honey?

Sun bear

All of them do! Sun bears love honey so much they are sometimes called honey bears. They tear open bees' nests with their long claws and lick up the honey. Sun bears are only the size of big dogs, so they can easily climb trees to find nests.

Remember
Can you remember the names of the eight different kinds of bear?

which bear is grizzly?

The brown bears of North America are called grizzly bears. The name comes from the white tips to their brown hairs, which make them look old and grey. Grizzled comes from the French word *gris*, which means grey.

Grizzly bear

Angry bear!

An angry bear makes itself look big and frightening! It rears up on its back legs and shows off its sharp teeth and claws.

Are bears clever?

Bears are very intelligent animals. They have large brains, are very curious and are good at finding their way around. American black bears are thought to be the most intelligent of all the bears.

why is a polar bear white?

A polar bear is the same colour as the snow and ice where it lives. This helps it to hide from its prey, because it is hard to see against the white background. The hairs in its coat are not really white. They are hollow tubes, which look white when they reflect the light.

Polar bear

Ghost bear

what are ghost bears?

Some American black bears are born with a white coat, which makes them look like ghosts. These white ghost bears live only on a few islands in western Canada.

star bear!

Ancient Greeks believed that the Great Bear star pattern was placed in the sky by their chief god, Zeus.

which bear is famous?

The giant panda is famous as the symbol of the World Wide Fund for Nature (WWF). This rare bear was chosen partly because of its black-and-white fur. The symbol could be photocopied in black and white, without the need for any colours.

write
Think up a story about a ghost bear that lives in a zoo!

Why are moon bears naughty?

Moon bear

Moon bears often visit farmers' fields and steal their crops, such as maize (sweetcorn). The bears use their sharp teeth to tear the maize cobs off the stalks. Farmers often hunt or trap the bears to save their crops.

can people get close to bears?

Yes! Tourists can get close to polar bears near the town of Churchill in Canada. They travel in big, strong buses, which keep them safe from the powerful, curious bears.

Polar bear

panda peril!

Giant pandas have lost their homes because people have cut down the forests where they live. However, people are working hard to protect and save these bears.

why do bears eat rubbish?

People's rubbish contains lots of left-over food for bears to eat. A bear can smell the rubbish from a long way away and will return to it over and over again. When bears spend a lot of time near people, they lose their fear of humans and can become dangerous.

Draw

Design a poster to show why we need to look after bears and how we can help them.

quiz time

3. Do pandas ever stop eating?
page 168

Do you remember what you have read about bears? Here are some questions to test your memory. The pictures will help you. If you get stuck, read the pages again.

4. Which bear has the longest tongue?
page 169

1. Which bear is not a bear?

page 163

5. Are sloth bears noisy?

page 170

2. Are bears good at climbing trees?

page 166

6. Do bears have picnics?

page 173

7. Which bear builds a snow cave?

page 175

8. Why do bears feast in autumn?

page 175

9. How big are bear cubs?

page 177

10. Do bears give piggybacks?

page 178

11. Which bear is grizzly?

page 181

12. Why is a polar bear white?

page 182

13. Why do bears eat rubbish?

page 185

Answers

1. A koala
2. Yes, bears can scramble up tree trunks easily
3. Not very often
4. The sun bear
5. Yes – when they feed at a termite mound, the noise can be heard 100 metres away
6. Teddy bears might do, but real bears don't
7. The polar bear
8. Because there is lots of food for them to eat
9. They are only very small
10. Sloth bear mothers give the cubs piggybacks
11. The brown bear of North America, called the grizzly bear
12. If it can't be seen against the snow and ice, so it can hide from its prey
13. Rubbish contains lots of left-over food for them to eat

Big cats

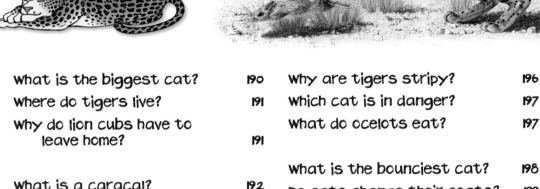

what is the biggest cat?

The Siberian tiger is the biggest cat, and one of the largest meat-eating animals in the world. The heaviest Siberian tiger was recorded at weighing 465 kilograms — that's the same weight as 23 of you! It also has thick fur to help it survive in freezing conditions.

Where do tigers live?

Tigers only live in southern and eastern Asia, in forests, woodlands and swamps. They used to live in much larger areas, but humans have now built houses and farms on much of the land. Siberian tigers live in snow-covered forests where temperatures can be −50°C.

Hair-head!

Male lion cubs begin to grow thick fur around their head and neck at about three years old. This fur is called a mane.

Siberian tiger

Why do lion cubs have to leave home?

Male lion cubs don't get to stay with their family group or pride, they get pushed out at about three years old. By then they are old enough to look after themselves. Soon they will take over new prides and have their own cubs.

Discover

Tigers are only found in certain parts of the world. Look on a map and see if you can find them.

what is a caracal?

A caracal is a smaller type of wild cat that lives in hot, dry desert-like places. It hunts small animals, such as rats and hares, and can leap up to 3 metres high to catch a passing bird.

Caracal

Jaguar

Think

Jaguars are good swimmers. Can you think of some other animals that can swim?

Are jaguars good swimmers?

Jaguars are very good swimmers. Of all cats, they are the most water-loving. They like to live in swampy areas or places that flood during the rainy season, and they enjoy cooling off in rivers. Jaguars are mainly found in Central and South America.

Tiny kitty!

The black-footed cat of southern Africa is one of the smallest cats in the world. It's half the size of many pet cats.

Why do tiger cubs have to hide?

Tiger cubs hide behind their mothers for safety. Adult male tigers will kill any cubs that aren't their own. Less than half of the tiger cubs born in the wild live to the age of two years old.

why are tigers stripy?

Tigers are stripy to help them blend into their shadowy, leafy surroundings. Stripes also help to hide the shape of the tiger's body, making hunting easier. White tigers born in the wild are less likely to live as long as orange tigers because they do not blend in as well.

Tiger cubs

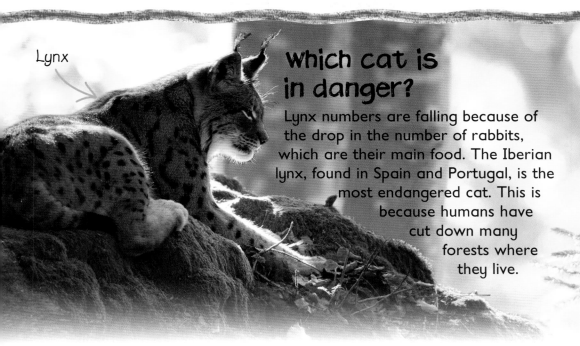

Lynx

which cat is in danger?

Lynx numbers are falling because of the drop in the number of rabbits, which are their main food. The Iberian lynx, found in Spain and Portugal, is the most endangered cat. This is because humans have cut down many forests where they live.

what do ocelots eat?

Ocelots, also called 'painted leopards', are small wild cats found mainly in South and Central America. They eat lots of different foods including rats, birds, frogs, monkeys, fish, tortoises and deer.

Think

How many types of food do you eat in a day? Is it as many as an ocelot?

Going, gone!

It's too late for some big cats. The Taiwan clouded leopard, and the Caspian, Bali and Javan tigers are extinct (have died out).

what is the bounciest cat?

The bounciest cat is the African serval. It can leap one metre high and travel 4 metres as it jumps. Unusually, it hunts in the day, for frogs, locusts and voles. Servals are like cheetahs, with slim, graceful, spotty bodies.

Serval

Do cats change their coats?

The lynx changes its coat with the weather. It lives in forests in northern Europe and Asia. In summer, the lynx's coat is short and light brown, but in winter its coat is much thicker, and light grey. This helps it to hide throughout the year.

paw prints!

The stripes on a tiger are a bit like our fingerprints – no two animals have exactly the same pattern on their coats.

why does a lion roar?

Lions roar to scare off other lions that stray onto their patch of land or territory. They also roar to let other members of their pride know where they are. A lion's roar is so loud it can be heard up to 10 kilometres away!

Roaring lion

wear

Cats are kept warm by their thick coats of fur. Put on some furry clothes. Do they keep you warm?

Why do leopards climb trees?

Leopards climb trees to rest or to eat their food in safety. These big cats often kill prey that is larger than themselves. They are excellent climbers and are strong enough to drag their prey up into a tree, away from other hungry animals.

Leopard

How can humans help big cats?

Humans can help big cats by protecting areas of rainforest and grassland where they live. These areas are called 'reserves'. In a reserve, trees are not allowed to be cut down and the animals can live in safety.

Puma

No boat? Float!

Ancient Chinese soldiers used blown-up animal skins to cross deep rivers. They used their mouths to blow in air, then covered them with grease to keep it in.

What is a puma's favourite food?

Rabbits, hares and rats are favourite foods for a puma. They will attack bigger animals too. In places where humans have built their homes near the puma's natural surroundings, people have been attacked by these cats.

can cheetahs run fast?

Yes they can — cheetahs are the world's fastest land animal. In a few seconds of starting a chase, a cheetah can reach its top speed of 105 kilometres an hour — as fast as a car! Cheetahs have 30 seconds to catch their prey before they run out of energy.

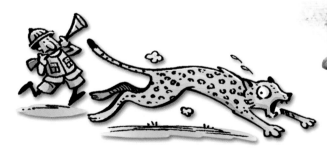

why do people hunt big cats?

Mainly for their beautiful fur. For many years, cats have been killed in their hundreds of thousands so that people can wear their skins. Tigers especially were hunted for their body parts, which were used in Chinese medicines.

Make

With a paper plate and some straws for whiskers, make a tiger mask. Cut out eyeholes and paint it stripy!

Can't catch me!

Even though cheetahs are super-fast runners, only half of their chases end with a catch. Sometimes they scare their prey off before they get close enough to pounce.

Cheetah

Tiger

what time do tigers go hunting?

Almost all cats, including tigers, hunt at night. It is easier for a tiger to creep up on its prey when there is less light. A tiger may travel many kilometres each night while hunting. Tigers hunt deer, wild pigs, cattle and monkeys.

where do cheetahs live?

Cheetahs live in grasslands called 'savannahs'. The savannah is dry, flat and open land, and is home to many other animals including gazelles, wildebeest and zebra. One of the best-known savannahs is the Serengeti in Africa.

Cheetahs hunting in the Savannah

why do cats wash their faces?

Cats wash their faces to spread their scent over their body. Cats have scent-producing body parts called glands on their chin. They use their paws to wipe the scent from their glands and when the cat walks, it can mark its area, or territory.

Lion

Play

With a friend, collect some pebbles and sticks and use them to mark out your own territories in your garden.

Slow down!

In the wild, cheetahs have a short lifespan. Their running speed gets a lot slower as they get older so they are less successful when they hunt.

How often do tigers eat?

Sometimes, tigers don't even eat once a week. When tigers catch an animal they can eat 40 kilograms of meat. They don't need to eat again for eight or nine days.

what is a group of cubs called?

A group of cubs is called a litter. There are usually between two and four cubs in every litter. Cubs need their mother's milk for the first few months, but gradually they start to eat meat. The young of some cats, such as the puma, are called kittens.

Mother puma and litter of kittens

Sharpen your claws!

Unlike other cats, a cheetah's claws don't go back into its paws. This is why they don't often climb trees – they find it hard to get back down.

Leopards fighting

Why do leopards fight each other?

Leopards fight each other to defend their territory. Each leopard has its own patch of land, which it lives in. Leopards use scent-marking and make scratches on certain trees to warn other cats away.

Draw
Many different animals live in trees. Draw some pictures of animals that live in trees near you.

Which cat lives in the treetops?

Clouded leopards are excellent climbers and spend much of their time in the treetops of their forest home. These animals have been seen hanging upside-down from branches only by their back legs. Clouded leopards are brilliant swimmers, too.

which big cats live in rainforests?

Tigers and leopards live in rainforests in India, and jaguars live in South American rainforests. Here, the weather stays hot all year, although there is often lots of rain.

Jaguar

what animals do jaguars hunt?

Young jaguars climb trees to hunt for birds and small animals. Adults are too heavy for the branches and hunt on the ground for deer, small mammals and sometimes cattle and horses.

Think

Are you as playful as the lion cubs? Invent some new games of your own to play with your friends.

Lion cubs

How do cubs learn to hunt?

Cubs learn to hunt by playing. Even a tortoise is a fun toy and by playing like this, cubs learn hunting skills. Many mothers bring their cubs a small, live animal so they can practice catching it.

It's a wrap!

The ancient Egyptians are well known for their 'mummies'. They even mummified animals including cats, birds and crocodiles.

HOW do snow leopards keep warm?

Snow leopards live on snowy mountains in Central Asia. To keep warm in winter they grow a thick coat of fur and store extra layers of fat under their skin. They also wrap their long tails around their bodies when they sleep to keep in heat.

Snow leopard

Which cat goes fishing?

The jaguar is an expert at fishing. Sometimes it waves its tail over the water to trick hungry fish before it strikes. Jaguars also fish for turtles and tortoises. Their jaws are so powerful that they can easily crack open a turtle shell.

Jaguar

Snowshoes!

Siberian tigers have large padded paws. They act as snowshoes and stop the tiger from sinking into the snow as it walks.

Make

Paint a picture of your favourite big cat. Make it as colourful as you like and give your big cat a name.

How do tigers stay cool?

Tigers such as the Bengal tiger live in places where it gets extremely hot in the summer. They can often be seen lying in pools of water to cool off, or resting in a shady area out of the hot sun.

which cat is the most mysterious?

The clouded leopard is the most mysterious cat. It is so shy and rare that it is unusual to spot one. Clouded leopards grow to 2 metres in length, half of which is its tail. It uses its tail to balance as it leaps through the trees.

Clouded leopard

Why do cats always land on their feet?

Cats have bendy bodies and strong muscles. If a cat, such as a caracal, falls from a tree it can twist its body round so that it can land on its feet. Its muscles and joints take in the shock of the ground for a soft landing.

A caracal lands on its feet

Big teeth!

The sabre-toothed cat really did exist, about 10,000 years ago. It was the size of a small lion and its teeth were 25 centimetres long!

How many babies do tigers have?

Tigers normally have between two and four babies called cubs. The mother tiger is pregnant for three months, and the cubs are born blind. Most births happen at night, probably because it is safer.

Measure

Using a measuring tape, see if you can measure how long a clouded leopard is.

why are cats the perfect hunters?

Because they have excellent eyesight and hearing, strong bodies and sharp teeth and claws. Many cats, such as lions, have fur that blends into their surroundings, which means they can hunt while staying hidden.

Lion hunting

How do cats see in the dark?

Cats have special cells at the back of their eyes that reflect light. They are able to see objects clearly even in dim light, which is why many cats hunt at night. Cats can see four times better in the dark than humans can.

Lioness at night

'Eye' can see you!

Cats have very good eyesight, in daylight and at night. For cats that live in grasslands, this helps them to spot distant prey on the open land.

Try

How well can you see in the dark? Turn off the light and wait for your eyes to adjust. Can you see anything?

Do big cats have enemies?

Big cats don't have many natural enemies. However, they watch out for animals, such as hyenas, that will gang up to steal their meal. A group of hyenas will attack and kill a big cat if it is weak or injured.

Quiz time

Do you remember what you have read about big cats? These questions will test your memory. The pictures will help you. If you get stuck, read the pages again.

page 197

3. Which cat is in danger?

page 197

4. What do ocelots eat?

page 190

1. What is the biggest cat?

page 198

5. What is the bounciest cat?

page 193

2. Are jaguars good swimmers?

page 201

6. How can humans help big cats?

7. Why do people hunt big cats?

page 202

8. What time do tigers go hunting?

page 203

9. Why do cats wash their faces?

page 205

10. Why do leopards fight each other?

page 207

page 212

11. Which cat is the most mysterious?

12. How many babies do tigers have?

page 213

13. Do big cats have enemies?

page 215

Answers

1. The Siberian tiger
2. Yes, they are
3. The lynx – especially the Iberian lynx
4. Rats, birds, frogs, monkeys, fish, tortoises and deer
5. The African serval
6. By creating protected reserves
7. For their fur
8. At night
9. To spread scent over their bodies
10. To defend their territories
11. The clouded leopard
12. Between two and four babies, or cubs
13. No, but hyenas can be a threat

Elephants

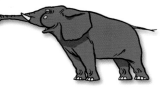

were mammoths woolly?

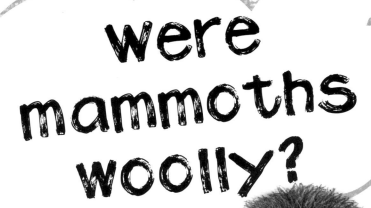

Woolly mammoth →

Yes, they had long, woolly fur to keep them warm in freezing weather. Mammoths were relatives of modern elephants and they lived thousands of years ago, when the world was much colder. Early people hunted mammoths for food, and for their thick fur.

220

How do we know about mammoths?

Because we have found their bodies frozen in ice. The freezing temperatures allowed the bones, hair and skin of some mammoths to remain almost the same for thousands of years.

Ancient art!

Long ago, people lived in caves. They painted animals, including mammoths, on the stone walls of their caves.

Paint

Make your own cave art. Paint mammoths, bears and wolves onto a big piece of strong paper or card.

Did elephants live with dinosaurs?

No, elephants came along millions of years after dinosaurs. The earliest elephants were a family of animals that looked like big pigs with long noses. Over time these animals changed and became the elephants we know today.

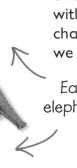

Early elephants

why are elephants so big?

Being big helps elephants to reach lots of tasty leaves in the trees. It also keeps them safe — not many animals would dare to attack such a huge beast! Elephants are the biggest animals that live on land, but their closest relatives are animals no bigger than rabbits.

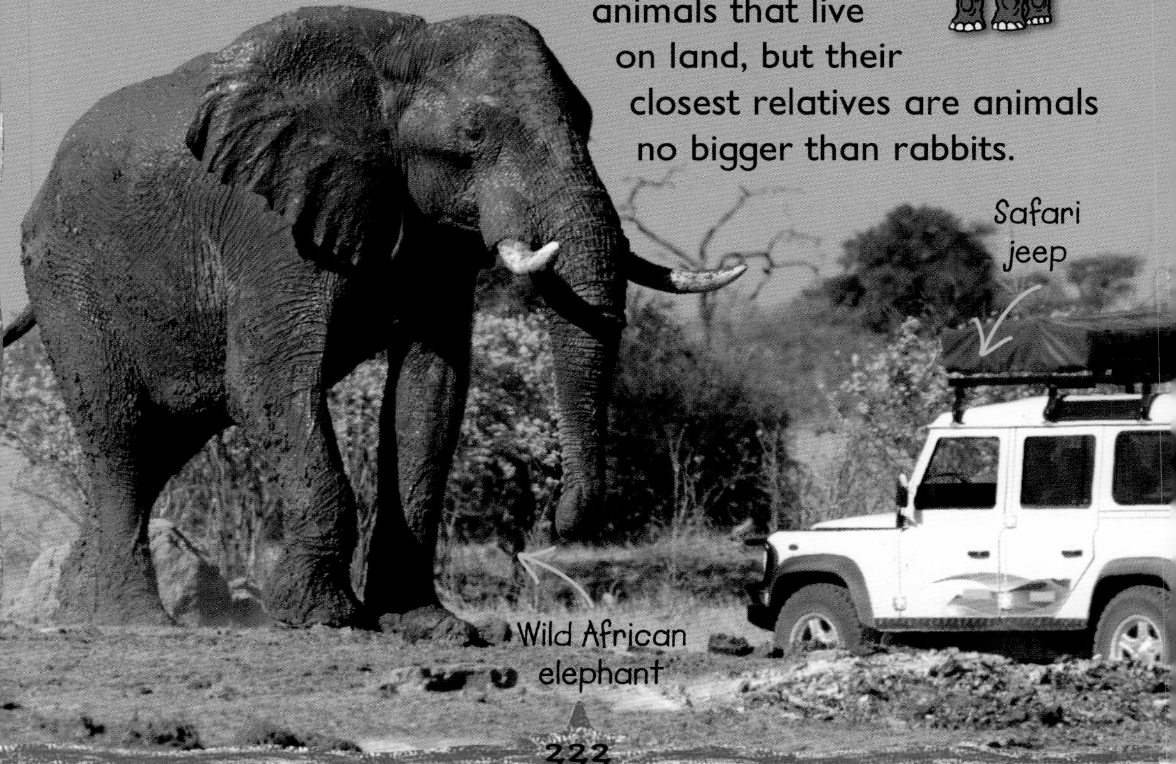

Safari jeep

Wild African elephant

Do elephants have families?

Yes, and their family groups are called herds. A herd is made up of baby elephants and their mothers, aunts and grandmothers. The oldest female elephant is in charge of the herd. Adult male elephants live alone.

Herd of elephants

Greedy guts!

Elephants have to spend most of the day eating. They munch up to 200 kilograms of grass, leaves, flowers and fruits every day.

what is a baby elephant called?

A baby elephant is called a calf. Elephant calves are playful and they have lots of things to learn, such as how to use their trunks. They stay close to their mothers until they are around four years old.

Find out

What animals will these babies grow up to be?
Kitten Puppy Lamb Gosling

Are all elephants the same?

No, there are three different types. Two live in Africa and one lives in Asia. African bush elephants live in grasslands. African forest elephants have hairy trunks and dark skin, and live in forests. Asian elephants are smaller than their African relatives and have smaller ears.

Asian elephants are 2 to 3.5 metres tall

African elephants can be 4 metres tall

Compare
Use a measuring tape to see how tall African and Asian elephants are. How tall are you?

How do baby elephants grow so strong?

They drink their mothers' milk — the perfect food for growing babies. A calf puts on up to 5 kilograms in weight every day. That is the same as five bags of sugar!

Calf drinking its mother's milk

Underwater!

Baby elephants can swim almost as soon as they can walk. They can even suckle (drink their mother's milk) while underwater.

Why do elephants pick up sticks?

Elephants pick up sticks with their trunks and use them to flick flies away, in the same way that humans use fly swats. Some elephants also use sticks to play with, scratch their backs or to doodle in the sand!

Why do elephants trumpet?

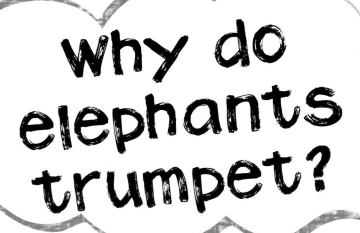

To talk to each other. An elephant makes a loud trumpeting sound by blasting air through its trunk. This tells other elephants that it is angry, scared or excited. Elephants also use rumbles, snorts and groans to 'talk' to each other.

Trunk

Do elephants get itchy?

Yes, especially if they have ticks. These little bugs suck their blood, making their skin sore. Elephants rub against trees until the ticks fall off. They also use their trunks to blow dust over their skin to stop the ticks biting.

scratch

Try scratching like an elephant. Rub your back against the edge of a door. Did it work?

Elephant rubbing on a tree

How do elephants help vets?

Elephants can help vets (animal doctors) get close to dangerous wild animals. When a rhino is ill, it is more likely to attack. By sitting on an elephant's back, a vet can get close enough to give it medical care.

Trumpet!

An elephant can trumpet so loudly that its call can be heard up to 10 kilometres away.

Do angry elephants flap their ears?

Yes, this is one way elephants show each other that they are not happy. Angry elephants also stamp the ground and shake their heads. This warns other animals — and people — to go away, or face big trouble!

Two elephants fighting

Try

Look in the mirror and see if you can move your ears without touching them. It might take practise!

Why are tusks like weapons?

Male elephants use their tusks like weapons to fight each other. Tusks are just overgrown teeth, but a stab from one can be deadly. The elephant with the biggest tusks usually wins the battle.

Get out of the way!

When a group of elephants run, it is called a stampede. A herd of stampeding elephants tramples anything in its path.

When do calves start to walk?

Elephant calves can walk when they are just 30 minutes old. The baby grows inside its mother for nearly two years. At birth, a calf is one metre tall and weighs the same as a man!

where do elephants go to drink?

Elephants walk a long way to find places to drink called waterholes. These are dips in the ground where water collects. Elephants drink what they need, and splash around to stay cool. Like other animal visitors to the waterhole, elephants graze on plants that grow nearby.

Giraffe

Elephant

Zebras

Waterhole

Which elephant can fly?

Dumbo can! He is a young elephant in the Disney movie. As a baby, Dumbo gets teased by the other elephants in the circus because he has huge ears. In the end, Dumbo realizes he can fly using his ears as wings.

Mould

Use plasticine to mould an elephant. Stand it on some foil for water – like it's at a waterhole.

Why do elephants roll in mud?

Elephants like to get covered in mud because it protects their skin from the Sun. It also stops insects from biting. Once elephants have cooled off in the waterhole, they often roll in mud at the edge and get dirty again!

Elephant splashing in the mud

Are trunks sensitive?

Yes – they are super-sized noses that can pick objects up. Elephants also use their trunks to communicate. They put their trunks in each other's mouths to say 'hello'. Mothers gently stroke their calves with their trunks to reassure them and to bond with them.

Mother and calf touching trunks

Do elephants have teeth?

Yes, they do. An elephant's teeth are big and strong – one tooth can be bigger than a man's shoe! An elephant has six sets of teeth during its life – a human only has two.

Count

How many teeth do you have? Find out how many teeth grown-ups have too. Who has more?

An elephant's back teeth

Can elephants hear with their feet?

Yes they can. Elephants make deep rumbling sounds, which travel through the ground. Other elephants feel the sounds with their feet. The sounds travel through the elephants' bones to its ears, so they can hear the noise.

Toothless!

Older elephants may die when their last set of teeth wears out because they can no longer eat.

Are elephants smart?

Elephants are very smart, and they can learn new skills. Some Asian elephants have learnt how to hold paintbrushes in their trunks and paint pictures! Others have worked out how to turn on taps, open gates and whistle.

Learn

Can you learn a new skill? Try painting a picture – but holding the brush in your mouth!

Asian elephant painting →

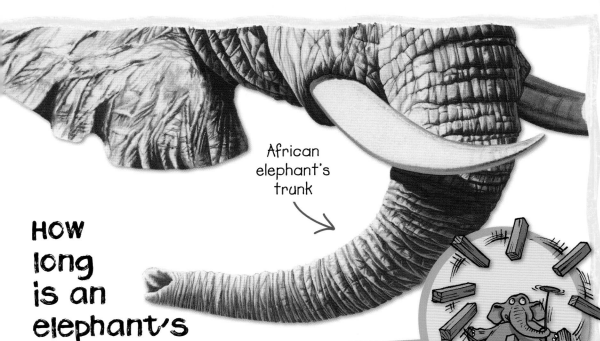

African elephant's trunk

HOW long is an elephant's trunk?

Male African elephants have the longest trunks, growing to 2 metres in length. That's about the same as a man's height! African elephants have two tips on the end of their trunk, but Asian elephants only have one tip.

Ta-da!

In the past, elephants were trained to perform tricks in circuses. They have also been used to carry heavy loads into war.

Skunk

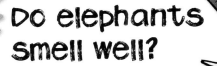

Do elephants smell well?

Yes! An elephant's trunk can smell other animals from far away. They hold their trunks up high to sniff the air. Male elephants also use their sense of smell to find females at mating time.

Why do elephants chew bark?

Chewing bark takes hours, but it is full of goodness. Grass tastes better, but when there is not much around, elephants eat bark, branches and even roots. Some trees are poisonous and calves learn not to eat them by copying their mothers and aunts.

Elephant chewing bark

Think
Vegetables are foods that are full of goodness. How many different types can you think of?

Which birds stand on elephants?

Birds called egrets stand on elephants' heads to enjoy some tasty snacks! Egrets feast on the flies and other bugs that buzz around elephants. The elephants don't mind the birds because they get rid of their annoying pests!

Egret

Don't make me mad!

An angry elephant uses its tusks to attack and stab. A single elephant is so strong that it could flip a car over with its tusks!

Do elephants chase animals?

Sometimes an elephant will chase an animal away if it feels scared by it. A mother elephant may charge if she thinks her calf is in danger. Angry adult elephants have been know to kill baboons, lions and even people.

Charging elephant

Baboon

Do elephants go swimming?

Even though they are huge, elephants are good swimmers. They use their trunks like snorkels, so they can breathe air even when their heads are underwater. Some elephants roll right over so only their feet poke out of the water.

Elephant swimming

Find out

The biggest animal in the world is an excellent swimmer. Can you find out what it is?

why do elephants have big ears?

Elephants live in hot countries and big ears help them to cool down. As they gently flap their ears, the moving air cools the blood inside. The cooled blood then moves around the rest of the elephant's body.

Do elephants remember?

They seem to. When elephants pass the bones of one of their herd, they stop and touch them with their trunks. They seem to be remembering their relative. Elephants can also remember where waterholes are and where to find good food.

watch out!

The deadly venom of a king cobra snake is strong enough to kill an elephant – the largest land mammal.

Elephants touching bones

Which huge elephant was famous?

Jumbo was the most famous elephant ever, and one of the largest. He was captured in 1861 and kept in zoos and a circus. Jumbo reached 4 metres in height! This is why people use the word 'jumbo' to mean big.

Jumbo the elephant

why do elephants march?

Elephants go on long walks, or marches, to look for food and water. After a rainy season, herds march to places where they know the plants they eat will be growing. Walking in a big group also helps to keep the herd safe from predators.

Mmm...salty!

Some elephants walk into caves searching for salt, which they lick off the cave walls! Salt is a mineral that elephants need to keep healthy.

Make

Ask an adult to help you cut an elephant shape out of card with four holes where its legs are. Put your fingers through the holes to make it march!

Is elephant dung tasty?

To some animals it is! Elephant dung is full of plants that haven't been digested (broken down). Animals such as baboons, warthogs and birds sort through the dung to find seeds, grass and pieces of fruit to eat.

Baboon eating elephant dung →

Do mothers protect their babies?

Yes, mother elephants guard their calves. Sometimes calves need to take a nap, so the rest of the mothers in the herd stand over them. Their shadows keep the babies cool as they snooze. The mothers keep watch for lions that could attack.

Mother elephants

Sleeping calf

Elephant sanctuary

What is an elephant sanctuary?

It is a safe place where elephants are protected. Sick elephants can be taken to a sanctuary, as well as young elephants who have lost their mothers. Once an elephant is old enough or well again it can be released back into the wild.

Handy noses!

Trunks are very handy. Elephants use them for holding and grabbing things, as well as greeting each other and fighting.

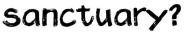

Search

Find out more about elephant conservation (keeping elephants safe) and how people can help them.

Why did elephants go to war?

Long ago, before the days of tanks and planes, elephants were sometimes used in wars. Soldiers were safer high up on an elephant's back, and it gave them a good view of their enemy's army.

Quiz time

Do you remember what you have read about elephants? Here are some questions to test your memory. The pictures will help you. If you get stuck, read the pages again.

3. How do baby elephants grow so strong?

page 225

4. Why do elephants pick up sticks?

page 225

1. Were mammoths woolly?

page 220

5. Why are tusks like weapons?

page 229

6. Can people ride on elephants?

page 230

2. What is a baby elephant called?

page 223

246

7. How much do elephants weigh?

page 231

8. Are trunks sensitive?

page 234

9. Why do elephants chew bark?

page 238

10. Which birds stand on elephants?

page 239

11. Do elephants remember?

page 241

12. Why do elephants march?

page 243

13. What is an elephant sanctuary?

page 245

Answers

1. Yes, they had long, woolly fur for warmth
2. A calf
3. They drink their mother's milk, which is the perfect food for growing babies
4. To flick flies away, scratch or doodle in the sand
5. Male elephants use them to fight each other
6. Yes, Asian elephants sometimes carry tourists
7. Males weigh up to 6 tonnes, and females weigh about half of this
8. Yes, trunks are very sensitive
9. Because it is full of goodness
10. Egrets
11. They remember where to find water and food, and may remember their dead relatives
12. Elephants march to look for food and water
13. A place where elephants are protected

what is a primate?

Monkeys and apes are primates. They have big brains and are very clever. Most primates are furry. They have hands with thumbs and fingernails. Humans are primates too.

Spider monkeys

cry baby!

Bushbabies are noisy primates that live in forests. When they make loud calls to each other, they sound like crying babies.

Spell
How many words can you make using the letters in the word PRIMATE?

Are monkeys like spiders?

No — but one type is called a spider monkey! It was given its common name because it has long, thin limbs — like a spider's legs.

Do monkeys and apes have tails?

Monkeys have tails, but apes don't. Tails help monkeys to climb and keep their balance. Apes are usually larger than monkeys and they also have bigger brains. Gorillas, chimpanzees (chimps), bonobos, orang-utans, gibbons and humans are apes.

Orang-utan

Do primates stay awake all night?

Nocturnal primates do! Animals that are nocturnal sleep during the day and wake up at sunset. Tarsiers have big eyes to help them see in the dark. They can turn their heads right round, so they can see what's behind them.

← Tarsier

Do bonobos like to play?

Bonobos love to play! Some bonobos living in a zoo play their own game of 'blind man's bluff'! They cover their eyes and try to walk without bumping into things.

Which lemur has a stripy tail?

Ring-tailed lemurs have long, bushy tails with black-and-white stripes. The males have smelly tails, and when they fight they wave them at each other.

Ring-tailed lemur

Hold tight!

Lemurs run and jump through trees. Babies have to grip tightly to their mothers' fur so they don't fall off!

why do chimps lick sticks?

Because they get covered with juicy termites!
Chimps poke sticks into big termite nests. The insects swarm over the sticks, which the chimps then pull out so they can lick up the tasty termites.

Chimps →

Sign
Use the Internet to discover how to sign for 'drink' and 'thank you'.

Greedy monkey!
Barbary macaques have large cheek pouches. When they find food, they stuff it into their pouches and save it for later.

Do chimps like to chatter?

Some do! A chimp called Washoe learnt how to use sign language to talk. She used her hands to make signs for lots of words, such as 'drink' and 'food'.

Squirrel monkey

Why do monkeys sleep in trees?

Monkeys can hide in a tree's branches, so they feel safer in trees than on the ground. Animals that want to eat other animals are called predators. The predators of squirrel monkeys include eagles, baboons and prickly porcupines.

Do apes love their mums?

Yes! All ape babies need their mums to look after them, but orang-utan babies need their mums the most. They stay with their mothers until they are eight years old. That's longer than any other primate, apart from humans.

Orang-utan and baby

Why does an aye-aye have a long finger?

An aye-aye has a long finger to get to tasty grubs. These little primates tap trees with their fingers. If they hear a grub moving inside, they make a hole and pull it out with their extra-long middle finger.

Aye-aye

What a racket!

Some mangabeys make a 'honk-bark' noise. Others 'whoop' to call each other and make a 'gobble' sound to say who they are.

Why do orang-utans climb trees?

Orang-utans climb trees to play amongst the branches, to find fruit to eat and to stay safe. Predators such as tigers, leopards and crocodiles hunt orang-utans.

Make

Who looks after you? Create them a beautiful card to say 'thank you'.

Why do chimps kiss?

Chimps can be very loving to members of their family. They like to sit together and kiss, stroke and groom each other. If chimps are annoyed they cough, but if they are very angry they bark, cry and scream.

Chimps →

Do primates use tools?

Some primates use tools to help them get food. Capuchin monkeys use heavy rocks to crack open hard nuts. Apes can use tools too, and they even teach each other how to use rocks to open nuts.

Brown capuchin

Time for change!

People love to watch chimps. Sadly, some chimps are taken from the wild to be put in zoos or even sold as pets.

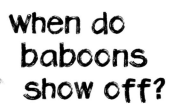

Discover

Use books and the Internet to find other animals that use tools.

When do baboons show off?

Male baboons love to show off when there are females about. They swagger around to show off their big muscles, long fangs and fine fur.

Do primates help forests to grow?

Yes they do! By eating plants and fruits, primates shape the trees and bushes. They also spread plant seeds in their poo. Primate poo puts goodness into the soil and helps new plants to grow.

Macaque $\longrightarrow$

why is a slow loris slow?

A slow loris likes to take life at a gentle pace. Moving slowly saves energy, so you don't need to find lots of food. It also helps an animal to stay hidden from predators.

Slow loris

Race

Have a slow race with a friend. The last person to finish is the winner!

watch out bugs!

Slow-moving primates can creep up on their prey, such as insects, and pounce at the last second.

when do monkeys fall out of trees?

When they get too greedy! Bird eggs are a special treat for primates. Smart birds build their nests on slender branches where monkeys can't reach them.

How fast can a gibbon swing?

Gibbons move faster than any other primate. They can swing through trees at great speed — up to 56 kilometres an hour. Gibbons can cover up to 15 metres in just one swing.

Gibbons

Crab-eating macaque

Do monkeys eat crabs?

Some monkeys will eat almost anything they can find! Crab-eating macaques live in swamps and they will grab crabs and frogs out of shallow water. Sometimes they just drop into the cool water for a swim.

Do primates have hands and feet like us?

Instead of paws and claws, primates have fingers, toes and flat fingernails just like us. This means they can grab hold of branches and delicately pinch small things.

Count
If one macaque can catch five crabs, how many can three macaques catch?

Super movers!
Spider monkeys are some of the fastest primate climbers. They have very long arms, legs and tails.

Which monkey is the biggest?

Male mandrills are the world's biggest monkeys. They are also the most colourful of all furry animals. Mandrills have enormous fangs that can grow to nearly 7 centimetres in length. Males are twice as big as females.

← Mandrill

Why do chimps pull faces?

Chimps pull faces to show how they are feeling. They pout when they want attention, open their lips when they are playful and bare their teeth when they are worried.

Pout

Try out some chimp faces in front of a mirror. Make an angry face too.

Pouting face

Worried face

Play face

Go wild!

Beautiful golden tamarins were once popular zoo animals, but now they are being released back into the wild so they can live free.

which monkey has a moustache?

Emperor tamarins have big white moustaches. Other tamarins have golden fur, crowns of white hair, beards or hairy ears. Tamarins live in South America.

Do monkeys change colour?

Silvered langurs do! These monkeys have silver-grey fur, but their babies are born bright orange. After three months, grey fur begins to grow. No one knows why the babies are orange, but it may remind older monkeys to be gentle with them.

Silvered langur

Silvered langur baby →

which ape has a colourful bottom?

A healthy male mandrill baboon has a brightly coloured bottom. Their bald bottoms have blue, pink or lilac skin. Female baboons often have pink or bright red bottoms.

A handy tail!

Monkeys use their tails like an extra arm or leg. They can hang from branches using their tails.

why does a sifaka skip?

Skipping is a fast way for sifakas (a type of lemur) to travel. They stand upright, with their arms stretched out, and skip sideways, scooting across the ground. Sifakas stick their tails out so they don't fall over as they hop, bound and leap.

Imagine
Pretend to be a sifaka and skip about!

Sifaka

How big is a gorilla?

Adult male gorillas are very big. They are called silverbacks, and they are up to 180 centimetres in height and weigh about 300 kilograms. That's the same weight as almost four people!

Silverback gorilla

Measure

Use a measuring tape to find out how tall a gorilla is.

what is the ugliest monkey?

Red uakaris (say: wak-ar-ees) are one of the ugliest monkeys. When they are born, baby uakaris have grey faces, but they turn bright red as they get older.

Bathtime fun!

Suryia the orang-utan lives in a wildlife park. He loved splashing in the bath and was taken to a pool. Suryia can now swim underwater!

Red uakari

why do gorillas beat their chests?

When a silverback gorilla stands up and beats his chest, it is time to get away fast! This is his way of warning you that he is getting angry and might attack.

HOW do bonobos keep clean?

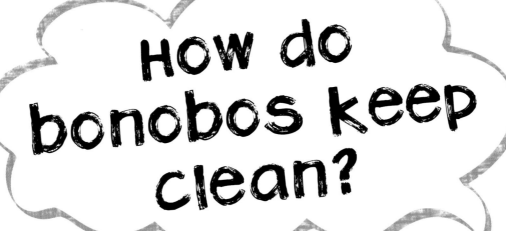

Bonobos spend lots of time cleaning each other's fur. They pick out bits of dirt, dead skin and even insects. This is called grooming and it is an important way for apes to make friends.

Bonobos

Do baboons have manes?

Male hamadryas baboons have large manes of hair that make them look big. Ancient Egyptians thought the silver-white manes made the baboons look sacred, or holy.

Scoop and sip!

Some baboons dig holes by ponds and let water flow into them. The water is clean enough to drink, with no nasty bugs in it.

Think

Can you think of any other animals that have manes of hair or fur?

Which orang-utan is in a film?

King Louie is one of the cartoon stars of a Disney film called *The Jungle Book*. He loves to sing, dance and play practical jokes. The story is based in an Indian jungle, but orang-utans don't really live in India.

King Louie

Baloo

which monkey has a big nose?

In Southeast Asia there are small monkeys with big noses. They are called proboscis monkeys (say: prob-os-kis), because proboscis is another word for 'nose'. The males have the biggest noses of all. When they run, their noses flop up and down!

Proboscis monkeys

Make
Use card and coloured pens to create a monkey mask.

Why do De Brazza's monkeys have white beards?

To scare other monkeys! De Brazza's monkeys also have long fangs. When they open their mouths wide, the white beards and long teeth make them look scary.

Go ape!

Every year, people all over the world dress up as gorillas and run 7 kilometres. They raise money to save the few gorillas that still live in the wild.

De Brazza's monkey

How do orang-utans stay dry?

Orang-utans live in tropical forests where it rains a lot every day. These clever apes use big leaves like umbrellas, and hold them over their heads to keep dry!

HOW do monkeys keep warm?

Most monkeys live in warm places.
Japanese macaques live in mountainous
areas where the weather can turn very cold.
They keep warm by soaking in pools of hot
water that bubble up from the ground.

Japanese
macaques

Bushbaby

why do bushbabies leap?

Bushbabies leap to catch their prey. They are fast movers, and can even take scorpions and spiders by surprise. In just one leap, a bushbaby can cover 10 metres!

Think

Can you work out how many metres a bushbaby would cover in three leaps?

LUCKY for some!

Only some lucky Japanese macaques have hot springs to soak in. Others have to huddle together to keep warm when cold winds bring snow.

which primate has two tongues?

Bushbabies use two tongues to eat gum, which comes from trees. They use their teeth to scrape the gum from the bark, then wipe it off their teeth with the special second tongue.

Quiz time

Do you remember what you have read about monkeys and apes? Here are some questions to test your memory. The pictures will help you. If you get stuck, read the pages again.

3. Why do chimps lick sticks?

page 254

4. Why does an aye-aye have a long finger?

page 257

1. Do bonobos like to play?

page 253

page 259

5. When do baboons show off?

2. Which lemur has a stripy tail?

page 253

6. Why is a slow loris slow?

page 261

7. Do monkeys eat crabs?

page 263

11. Do baboons have manes?

page 271

8. Which monkey has a moustache?

page 265

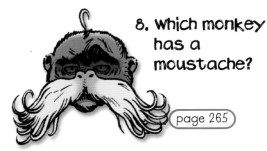

12. Which monkey has a big nose?

page 272

13. How do monkeys keep warm?

page 274

9. Why does a sifaka skip?

page 267

10. What is the ugliest monkey?

page 269

Answers

1. Yes they do. Some even play games of blind man's buff!
2. The ring-tailed lemur
3. Because they get covered with termites when chimps poke them into big termite nests
4. To get to tasty grubs in trees
5. When there are females about
6. To save energy and stay hidden from predators
7. Crab-eating macaques do
8. An emperor tamarin
9. Skipping is a fast way for them to travel
10. The red uakari
11. Male hamadryas baboons do
12. The proboscis monkey
13. Japanese macaques keep warm by soaking in pools of hot water that bubble up from the ground

Deadly creatures

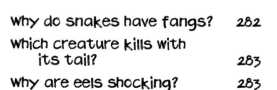

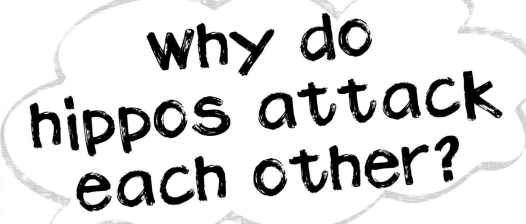

Why do hippos attack each other?

Male hippos attack each other to defend the patch of land where they live. When they fight, hippos stand face-to-face with their mouths wide-open, and slash and swipe at each other with their tusk-like teeth. Sometimes these fights end in the death of one, or both of the hippos.

Hippos

which bird can kill while it flies?

Lots of birds hunt 'on the wing'. The peregrine falcon is the fastest hunting animal in the world and dives at 230 kilometres an hour. It chases its prey before attacking it to tire it out.

Peregrine falcon

Hold it, hippopotamus!

Hippos and whales are closely related – maybe this is why hippos can hold their breath under water for 12 minutes!

Do army ants go hunting?

Army ants hunt in groups, sometimes of more than one million ants. They move forward in a wave across the ground. Ants at the front of the group kill insects and small lizards in their path, while ants further back carry food to the nest.

Army ants

Explore

Ants live in most places, even in your garden. Take a look outside and see if you can spot any.

why do snakes have fangs?

Poisonous snakes such as rattlesnakes have an extra-long pair of teeth called fangs. A deadly poison called venom runs along a groove in each fang. When the snake bites an animal, its fangs sink into the animal's skin and venom is injected.

Rattlesnake

which creature kills with its tail?

All scorpions have a poisonous sting in their tail. They use their front claw-like arms to hold their prey, while their tail-sting injects a harmful venom. Few scorpions can badly injure a human, but a sting from the death stalker scorpion can kill.

Common yellow scorpion

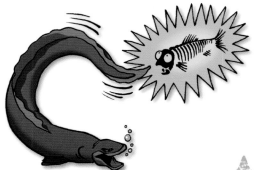

Death match!

Scorpions normally live alone because most of them eat other scorpions. If two scorpions meet, they will fight to the death and the loser is eaten by the winner.

Why are eels shocking?

Electric eels use electricity to zap their prey and to attack other animals that threaten them. The electric eel, which is actually a type of fish, can produce up to 600 volts of electricity – enough to kill a human!

Discover

Some eels use electricity to hunt. What things in your home use electricity?

which deadly fish looks like a stone?

The stonefish looks just like a piece of coral-covered rock or stone on the seabed. It sits and waits for its prey to come close. Then the stonefish strikes out at lightning speed and gobbles up its victim. For defence, the stonefish is covered in poisonous spikes.

Stonefish

Hornet

can insects be deadly?

Many insects can harm other animals. Bees, wasps and hornets have stings in their tails that can inject venom. A sting from one of these insects can cause swelling and pain, and rarely even death.

King sting!

The world's largest hornet is the Asian giant hornet. Its body is up to 4.5 centimetres long and its stinger is 6 millimetres long.

Remember

If you are stung by an insect tell an adult straight away because some stings can make you feel unwell.

what do animals use their tusks for?

Tusks are overgrown teeth, and animals such as walruses and elephants use their tusks as weapons to stab and swipe at attackers. Males use them to fight one another during the mating season.

why do crocodiles have big teeth?

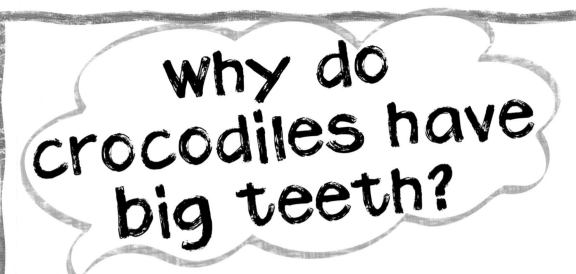

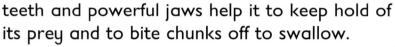

Crocodiles have lots of big teeth for catching their prey. A crocodile's diet includes fish, birds and mammals, such as gazelle and wildebeest. The crocodile's sharp teeth and powerful jaws help it to keep hold of its prey and to bite chunks off to swallow.

Nile crocodile

Do snakes eat people?

Pythons, such as Burmese pythons, have been known to attack and kill humans — but rarely. These snakes usually eat small mammals and birds, but can open their mouths wide enough to swallow animals such as pigs and deer whole!

Burmese python

Boiled eggs!

Whether a baby crocodile is a female or a male depends on temperature. A female will develop in a warm egg and a male will develop in a cool egg.

Make

Using an old sock for the body, buttons for eyes and wooden pegs for teeth, make a crocodile glove puppet.

Gazelle

What is a deathspin?

A deathspin is what crocodiles and alligators do to drown their prey. A crocodile pulls its victim underwater and twists and turns until the animal is dead. The crocodiles' strong jaws keep a grip on the animal as it rolls and turns in the water.

what is a black widow?

The black widow is one of the world's most deadly spiders. Black widows only bite if they are disturbed. Male black widows are harmless, but a bite from a female can kill a human. Sometimes, the female black widow eats the male after mating.

Black widow

Why do fish bite?

Piranhas are small fish with razor-sharp teeth. They can be very fierce and will bite anything that they think they can eat. Piranhas usually hunt alone but may gather in groups to attack larger animals, which they strip to the bone in minutes.

Piranhas feeding

A bite to eat!

Piranhas are found in rivers in South America and are often caught for food by the local people. Their teeth are used in weapons and tools.

Why do crocodiles eat rotting meat?

Crocodiles eat rotting meat because it is easier to swallow. Crocodiles and alligators store their food by wedging the dead animal under an underwater branch or log, so that it rots down. Sometimes, they store their food for several weeks.

which bat eats bones?

False vampire bats kill their prey by biting its head or neck and crushing its skull. Then it swallows the flesh, bones, teeth, fur and even feathers of its prey. Its favourite foods are birds, as well as lizards, frogs and mice.

False vampire bat

Flies for tea!

Most bats eat insects. They catch their prey by snatching it out of the air while flying. Some bats will catch around 2000 insects in one night!

which tiny jellyfish is deadly?

The Irukandji jellyfish can be found in the waters around Australia. It is very dangerous despite its small size – its body is the size of a small grape and its tentacles can give a deadly sting.

Irukandji jellyfish

Poison-dart frog

wear

Try on some colourful, bright clothes, like the poison-dart frog. How many colours are in your outfit?

why are some frogs brightly coloured?

The green poison-dart frog is brightly coloured to tell attackers to stay away. These frogs also make a poisonous slime on their skin. Local people of South America wipe the poison onto the ends of their hunting darts because it's strong enough to kill animals such as monkeys.

what is the deadliest lizard?

The Komodo dragon is the deadliest, and biggest, meat-eating lizard. It eats every part of an animal, including its bones. This lizard has a poisonous bite, so even if prey escapes, the Komodo dragon just follows it until it weakens and dies.

Komodo dragon

HOW do coyotes catch their prey?

Coyotes are fast runners and often chase speedy jackrabbits across rocks and up hills. When hunting larger animals such as deer, a group of coyotes chase the animal to tire it out and bite its neck to stop it breathing.

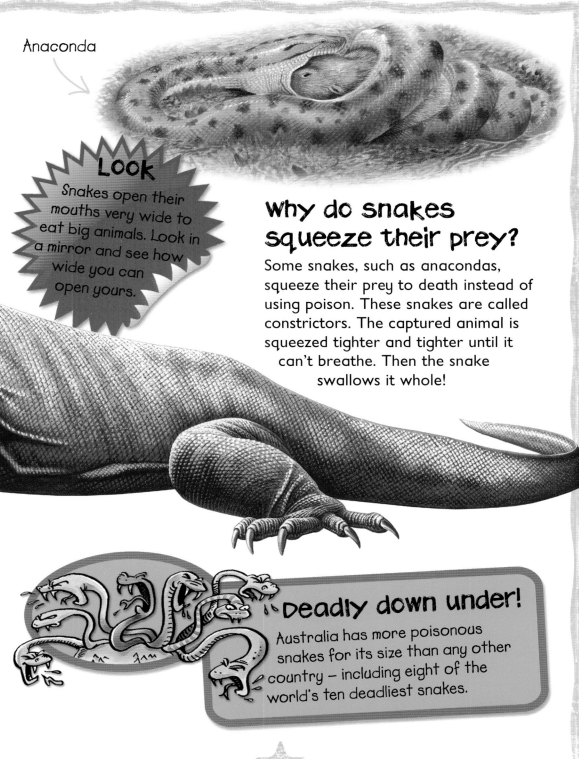

Anaconda

LOOK

Snakes open their mouths very wide to eat big animals. Look in a mirror and see how wide you can open yours.

Why do snakes squeeze their prey?

Some snakes, such as anacondas, squeeze their prey to death instead of using poison. These snakes are called constrictors. The captured animal is squeezed tighter and tighter until it can't breathe. Then the snake swallows it whole!

Deadly down under!

Australia has more poisonous snakes for its size than any other country – including eight of the world's ten deadliest snakes.

293

can monkeys be dangerous?

Mandrills are the biggest type of monkey, and they can be dangerous. Their fangs grow up to 7 centimetres long and are used as deadly weapons to attack weaker members of their group. Males also show their teeth to impress females during the mating season.

Draw

Using colouring pencils, draw a picture of a monkey. See if you can make it as colourful as this mandrill.

Mandrill

why do wolves snarl?

Wolves snarl when they are angry or threatened by another animal. When a wolf snarls, its lips curl back to show its long, sharp teeth and its nostrils widen. The fur on the wolf's back also stands on end to make it look bigger to an attacker.

Wolf

scary sound!

A wolf's growl is a very low, deep sound. They growl to threaten other wolves and to show they have power over a group of wolves, which is called a pack.

which shark gives a warning before it bites?

The grey reef shark does. If it feels threatened it drops its fins down and raises its snout so that its body is in an 'S' shape. Then it weaves and rolls through the water. If its warning is not taken, the shark will bite before swimming away.

which big cats hunt in teams?

Unlike most big cats, lions hunt as a team. Female lions, called lionesses, hunt for food while the males and cubs wait for their meal. A group of lionesses can catch large animals, including zebra, gazelle and wildebeest.

Lionesses hunting

which turtle has a deadly bite?

The alligator snapping turtle does. It has a 'beak' made of a tough material. It eats fish, which it lures in with its worm-like tongue, as well as crabs, clams and even other turtles!

Alligator snapping turtle

when are brown bears deadly?

Brown bears can be deadly if they are injured or weak, or if they are surprised by a human. A mother bear will also defend her cubs by attacking. In North America, a number of people have been killed by brown bears.

Think
Bears can be scary! Try to think of any friendly bears that appear in films and cartoons.

Deadly lure!
The alligator snapping turtle lures its prey into its mouth by wiggling its pink tongue!

Eagle owl

The eagle owl does.
Eagle owls hunt 'on the wing'
(while flying) for any kind of
bird, including other owls. As well
as hunting in the air, these owls
hunt on the ground for insects,
reptiles and mammals. The eagle
owl is the biggest owl.

what do fleas eat?

Fleas live on most furry animals, and sometimes humans. They jump from animal to animal feeding on blood and can spread disease. Fleas were responsible for spreading the 'black death', a disease that killed millions of people in the 14th century.

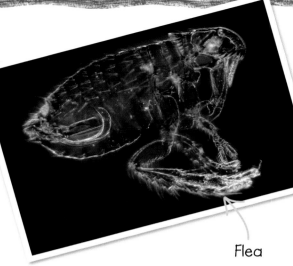

Flea

what is the deadliest octopus?

The blue-ringed octopus is the world's most dangerous octopus – and it's only 10 to 20 centimetres long. It grabs prey with its sticky tentacles and then gives a bite that injects venom. Its venom is strong enough to kill a human in four minutes!

Blue-ringed octopus

Silent hunter!

An owl's feathers have fluffy edges. This softens the sound of their wings flapping so they can swoop down on their prey in silence.

count

An octopus has eight tentacles. How many tentacles would three octopuses have?

HOW do funnel web spiders Kill?

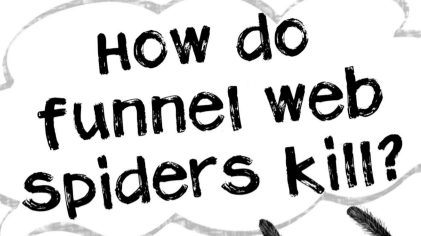

Funnel web spiders are poisonous and have large fangs that are strong enough to bite through your fingernail. They bite their prey many times, injecting a strong poison until their victim is dead. Funnel web spiders normally eat insects and small lizards.

Funnel web spider

Fighting elephants

when are elephants deadly?

During the breeding season, male elephants, called bulls, become aggressive and fight each other to win a female. One elephant is strong enough to flip over a car.

web-tastic!

There are about 20,000 types of spider that spin webs to catch their prey. Most of these make a new web every night, after they've eaten the old one!

Think

Can you puff like a puffer fish? Take a deep breath in. What happens to your body?

which fish can make itself spiky?

The poisonous puffer fish can make itself into a spiky ball when under attack. It gulps in water to make its body swell up and its spikes stand on end. Some chefs are trained to cook it. They learn which body parts to take out so it is safe to eat.

Are polar bears friendly?

Big, fluffy polar bears look friendly, but they are deadly killers. Young polar bears practise fighting skills to get ready for battles as adults over females. The bear's powerful bite and huge paws means it can kill its prey quickly.

Polar bears fighting

Which reptile squirts poison?

If attacked, the fire salamander squirts out a poison that is harmful to other animals. Fire salamanders look like a cross between a lizard and a frog, and they have colourful patterns on their skin to warn predators that they are poisonous.

Fire salamander

Burning hot!

The word 'salamander' means 'within fire' in Persian because a long time ago people thought that salamanders could walk through fire. However, this isn't true.

Colour

Draw an outline of a fire salamander and colour it in using five colours.

Why do rhinos charge?

Female rhinos protect their calves by charging at enemies. Rhinos have bad eyesight, but excellent senses of smell and hearing. They can quickly sense if there is a threat nearby. A charging rhino can reach a speed of 50 kilometres an hour!

Which deadly creature lives in a shell?

The cone shell is a type of snail that lives in the sea. Instead of chasing its prey, it sits and waits for creatures to come close. It has a long, tongue-like arm that it uses to shoot a poisonous dart into its victim.

Make

Using a cardboard box, make your own shell. Paint a pattern on it like the cone shell's.

Cone shell

Do killer bees really exist?

Yes, they do! A scientist tried to create bees that made more honey than normal, but instead he created 'killer bees'. They attack in large groups and around 1000 people have been killed by these minibeasts.

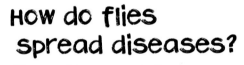

Delightful droppings!

Lots of insects find animal droppings delicious. Some beetles lay their eggs in steaming piles of droppings, so that when the eggs hatch, the young insects can eat the dung!

How do flies spread diseases?

Tsetse flies spread disease when they feed. They bite and suck blood from one animal and then another, leaving germs behind. These germs can cause 'sleeping sickness' in humans, which makes you want to sleep all the time.

Tsetse fly before feeding

Tsetse fly after feeding

Quiz time

page 284

Do you remember what you have read about deadly creatures? These questions will test your memory. The pictures will help you. If you get stuck, read the pages again.

3. Which deadly fish looks like a stone?

page 287

4. Do snakes eat people?

1. Which bird can kill while it flies?

page 281

page 288

5. What is a black widow?

6. Why do crocodiles eat rotting meat?

page 289

2. Which creature kills with its tail?

page 283

7. What is the deadliest lizard?

page 292

8. Which shark gives a warning before it bites?

page 295

page 296

9. Which big cats hunt in teams?

10. Which turtle has a deadly bite?

page 297

11. What is the deadliest octopus?

page 299

12. Which fish can make itself spiky?

page 301

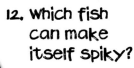

13. Do killer bees really exist?

page 305

Answers

1. The peregrine falcon
2. The scorpion
3. The stonefish
4. Some types of python have but this is very rare
5. One of the world's deadliest spiders
6. Because it is easier to swallow
7. The Komodo dragon
8. The grey reef shark
9. Lions do
10. The alligator snapping turtle
11. The blue-ringed octopus
12. The spiny puffer fish
13. Yes, they do

coral reef

what is a coral reef?

Coral reefs are living structures that grow in the sea. They are built by millions of tiny animals, called coral polyps. When they die, new polyps grow on top. This builds up layers of coral rock over time. Some reefs, such as the Great Barrier Reef, are enormous and can be seen from the air.

Great Barrier Reef

Coral

Do trees grow underwater?

Trees do not grow underwater, but soft tree corals look like trees because they have branches. Coral reefs are sometimes called 'rainforests of the sea'. Like rainforests on land, coral reefs are important homes for millions of marine animals.

Soft tree coral

Big brains!

Octopuses are super smart animals that live near reefs. They are experts at finding prey hiding in rocky crevices.

Colour!

Choose your favourite fish from this book. Copy it onto paper and colour it in.

How do coral polyps feed?

Coral polyps live in hard, stony cups and feed on tiny animals that drift by in the water. They catch food with tiny stingers on their tentacles, as do jellyfish, which are in the same animal family as coral polyps.

can turtles swim far?

Turtles go on very long journeys across the sea to feed, mate or lay their eggs. Female turtles always return to the same beach to lay their eggs. How they find their way is still a mystery, but they don't seem to get lost!

Discover
Use an atlas to find out which country beginning with 'A' is near the Great Barrier Reef.

Turtles from *Finding Nemo*

which deadly fish is hard to spot?

Stonefish are almost impossible to see when they are lying flat and still on the seabed. Their colours blend in with the rocky and sandy surfaces of the sea floor.

Stonefish

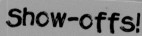

Show-offs!

Cuttlefish can change colour! In just a few seconds, a cuttlefish can flash colours of red, yellow, brown or black.

Do seahorses gallop?

Seahorses are fish, not horses, so they cannot run or gallop! They are not very good swimmers so they wrap their tails around seaweed to stop ocean currents carrying them away.

why are fish like lions?

Lionfish

Some fish are like lions because they hunt for food at night. Lionfish hide among rocks in the day. As the Sun sets, they come out to hunt for small animals to eat. They have amazing stripes and spines on their bodies. Their spines hold venom, which can cause very painful stings.

Dive but stay alive!
Divers can use cages to watch sharks safely. The divers wear masks and carry tanks that have air inside them so they can breathe underwater.

when do birds visit reefs?

Birds visit coral reef islands to build their nests. When their eggs hatch, the birds find plenty of fish at the reef to feed to their chicks. Albatrosses are large sea birds, so their chicks need lots of fish!

count

If an albatross chick needs to eat two big fish every day, how many fish will it eat in five days?

can slugs be pretty?

Yes they can! Like many coral reef animals, sea slugs have amazing colours and patterns. These warn other animals that they are harmful to eat. Most sea slugs are small, but some can grow to 30 centimetres in length.

Sea slugs

what lives on a reef?

A huge number of different animals live on or around reefs. They are home to fish of all shapes and sizes, including sharks. There are many other animals too – octopus, squid, slugs, sponges, starfish and urchins all live on reefs.

Black sea urchin

Sea turtle

Starfish

Do turtles lay eggs?

Yes, they do. Turtles spend most of their lives at sea, but lay their eggs on land. A female turtle digs a hole in the sand, and lays her round eggs inside it. When the eggs hatch, the baby turtles crawl back to the sea.

A sting in the tail!

Blue-spotted rays live in coral reefs and feed on shellfish, crabs and worms. They have stinging spines on their tails.

Measure

Every year coral reefs grow about 10 centimetres. How much have you grown in a year?

What do coral reefs need to grow?

The polyps that build up coral reefs need plenty of sunlight and clean water to grow. They mostly live in shallow water near land where sunlight can reach them.

Sea goldies

Bottlenose dolphins

Barracudas

Butterfly fish

Wobbegong shark

Whitetip reef shark

can parrots swim?

Of course not – parrots are birds that live in jungles! Parrotfish, however, are dazzling, colourful fish that swim around reefs, nibbling at the coral. They have beak-like mouths, which is why they are named after parrots.

Parrotfish

which animal looks like seaweed?

A type of seahorse called a leafy seadragon does! Its strange shape makes it hard to spot when it swims around seaweed, hiding it from big fish that might want to eat it.

Leafy seadragon

Think

Make up a story about a leafy seadragon and a parrotfish. Draw pictures to tell your story.

Do sponges help build reefs?

Sometimes – sponges are animals that bore, or dig, holes into coral. This can weaken a reef. However, when sponges die their bodies build up extra layers, which add to the reef structure.

Deadly jelly!

Box jellyfish have deadly stings on their tentacles. Divers and swimmers stay away from them.

why does an octopus have eight arms?

Having eight arms allows an octopus to move quickly and grab food to eat. Each arm has suction cups that can grip onto things. An octopus grabs food with its eight strong arms, and pulls it towards its mouth.

Make
Draw lots of pictures of coral reef animals and stick them on a large piece of card to make a poster.

Blue-ringed octopus

Who looks after a seahorse's eggs?

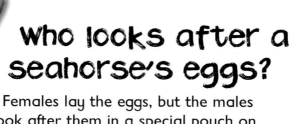

Females lay the eggs, but the males look after them in a special pouch on the front of their bodies. This keeps the eggs safe from bigger fish that might eat them. When the eggs hatch, the babies swim out of the pouch.

Don't eat me!

Little coral polyps live next to each other, but they do not always get on. Sometimes one polyp might eat its neighbour!

Do christmas trees grow on reefs?

Christmas trees do not grow on reefs – but Christmas tree worms do! These little animals live in burrows inside the reef. The feathery, spiral parts we can see are called feeding tentacles.

Christmas tree worm →

where do clownfish live?

Clownfish live in the tentacles of coral reef creatures called sea anemones. Like coral polyps, these strange-looking animals sting their prey. Clownfish have a slimy skin covering that protects them from the sting and allows them to live there unharmed.

Sea anemone

Hide

Invite some friends to join you in a game of hide and seek. Where could you hide?

Clownfish

See snakes? Swim!

Snakes don't just live on land. Some of the world's most deadly snakes live in the sea but come onto land to lay their eggs.

Which coral reef fish wears a crown?

The queen angelfish does! It has a blue-black spot, or 'crown' on its head. This pretty fish lives in the warm waters around Caribbean reefs. It is brightly coloured with yellow and blue patterns to help it blend in with its surroundings.

Queen angelfish

Which shrimp likes to punch its prey?

Mantis shrimps may be small, but they can pack a big punch. They live in reefs near Australia and in the Pacific Ocean. They punch their prey to stun them, and then tuck in for a tasty meal.

Why are corals different shapes?

The shape a coral grows into depends on the type of polyp it has. Where the coral grows on the reef is also important. Brain coral grows slowly and in calm water. Staghorn and elkhorn corals grow more quickly, and in shallow water.

Brain coral

Elkhorn coral

Staghorn coral

Are there butterflies in the sea?

There is a type of butterfly living in the sea – but it isn't an insect, it's a fish! Many butterfly fish have colourful spots and stripes to help make them hard to spot.

Butterfly fish

LOOK

Find out if you can see colours better in the dark or in the light.

Going for a spin!

Dolphins visit coral reefs to feast on fish. They jump out of the water and can even spin, though no one knows why they do it!

Can fish see in the dark?

Many animals can see in the dark! Lots of coral animals sleep during the day, but when the Sun goes down they come out to look for food or mates. Many of them, such as the red soldierfish, are much better at seeing in the dark than people are.

which crab moves house?

Hermit crabs live inside borrowed shells and move house if they find a bigger, better one. They don't have their own shells so they have to find one to protect their soft bodies. Most hermit crabs choose snail shells to live in.

Hermit crab

Damaged coral

why is some coral white?

Most coral is very colourful, until it dies and turns white or grey. There are many reasons why corals are dying. Dirty water is one of the most important reasons. Water that is too warm is also bad for polyps.

Slow-grow!
Giant clams can grow to be enormous — up to 150 centimetres long! They can live for 70 years.

Measure
Use a measuring tape to find out how long a giant clam is.

who looks after coral reefs?

Special ocean parks are set up to look after the animals that live on coral reefs. People are not allowed to catch the fish or damage the reef inside these protected areas.

How do fish clean their teeth?

They get other fish to do it for them! Little fish, called wrasses, eat the bits of food stuck in the teeth of other fish, such as moray eels. The wrasses get a tasty meal and the moray eels get their teeth cleaned!

Moray eel

Whale shark

Are all sharks dangerous?

No, most sharks would never attack a person. Whale sharks are huge but they don't eat big animals. They swim through the water with their large mouths open. They suck in water and any little creatures swimming in it.

Which crab wears boxing gloves?

Boxer crabs hold sea anemones in their claws, like boxing gloves. They wave them at any animals that come too close – the sight of the stinging tentacles warns other animals to stay away.

Brush

We don't have wrasses, so when you brush your teeth try hard to remove every tiny bit of food.

Wrasse

School's out!

A group of fish is called a shoal, or a school. Fish often swim in shoals because it helps them stay safe from bigger fish that might eat them.

Do sharks use hammers?

No, but some sharks have heads that look like hammers! These strange-looking sharks have wide, flattened heads. The shape might help them to find food, swim fast or change direction easily.

Hammerhead shark →

Do squid change colour?

Yes, squid and octopuses are able to change colour, so they can hide, or send messages to each other. They can change colour very quickly – in just one or two seconds!

Caribbean reef squid

world wonder

You can see the Great Barrier Reef from space! At over 2000 kilometres long, it is the largest structure ever built by living creatures

which fish are shocking?

Electric rays can shock other animals by making electric charges in their bodies. As they swim over other fish, they stun them with powerful jolts of electricity. The rays then eat their prey whole, headfirst!

Dress

We change the way we look with the clothes we wear. How quickly can you change clothes?

which fish is hard to eat?

Pufferfish are strange-looking, poisonous fish with sharp spines. When they feel scared, pufferfish blow up their bodies to make their spines stand on end. This makes them bigger and much harder to swallow.

Pufferfish with
spines relaxed

Pufferfish with
spines on end

March

Imagine you are a lobster on a long march. How far can you march before you get tired?

why do lobsters march?

Coral reef spiny lobsters march to deep, dark water where they lay their eggs. They march through the night at the end of the summer. Thousands of lobsters join the march to reach a safe place to breed.

Crown-of-thorns starfish

clean teeth!

When fish such as sweetlips want their teeth cleaned, they swim to find wrasse fish and open their mouths.

How do starfish eat their prey?

Starfish turn their mouths inside out to eat. The crown-of-thorns starfish kills coral by eating the soft polyps inside. Each of these large starfish can have up to 21 arms.

quiz time

3. Why are fish like lions?

page 314

Do you remember what you have read about coral reefs?
Here are some questions to test your memory. The pictures will help you. If you get stuck, read the pages again.

4. Do turtles lay eggs?

page 316

1. Do trees grow underwater?

5. Which animal looks like seaweed?

page 311

page 319

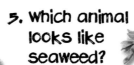

page 313

2. Which deadly fish is hard to spot?

6. Who looks after a seahorse's eggs?

page 321

7. Where do clownfish live?

page 322

11. Which crab wears boxing gloves?

page 331

8. Do jellyfish wobble?

page 325

12. Which fish are shocking?

page 333

13. Why do lobsters march??

page 335

9. Can fish see in the dark?

page 327

10. Who looks after coral reefs?

page 329

Answers

1. No, but some corals have branches like trees
2. When it is a stonefish
3. Because they are hunters and come out to feed at night
4. Yes
5. The leafy sea dragon
6. The male seahorse
7. In the tentacles of sea anemones
8. No, they are living animals and aren't made from jelly
9. Yes – many such as the red soldierfish can see well in the dark
10. Special ocean parks
11. The boxer crab
12. Electric rays
13. They march to an area where they can breed or lay their eggs

Endangered animals

what are endangered animals?

They are very rare animals that will die out soon without our help. If an animal, such as a tiger, is endangered it means there are very few of them left in the world and they are in danger of being wiped out completely.

Tigers

Philippine eagle

Do eagles need our help?

Yes they do. Eagles are having trouble surviving because we have built farms, mines and cities in their natural homes. Humans have also hunted and poisoned these rare birds, and collected their eggs.

Poo reveals all!

Endangered animals' poo reveals a lot about what they eat and how healthy they are. This information can help scientists to stop rare animals from dying out.

How many animals die out every day?

Up to 300 animal types probably die out every day — especially small ones such as bugs. About half of all the world's insects are in danger of dying out right now.

Draw

Can you think of five different bugs? Using books to help you, draw pictures of your five bugs.

Will I ever see a dinosaur?

Nobody will ever see a real living dinosaur. They died out millions of years before people lived on Earth. Dinosaurs ruled the world for over 150 million years and developed into over 1000 different types.

Tyrannosaurus rex

LOOK

Watch the birds in the sky. They probably developed from dinosaurs with feathers!

why did the dinosaurs die out?

It may have been because a huge space rock hit Earth. Dust thrown into the air would have blocked out the sunlight. The dinosaurs could not have survived because the animals that they ate would have also died out.

Going, going, gone!

More than 99 out of every 100 animals that ever lived are extinct and will never walk the Earth again.

Dodo

can we save the dodo?

No we can't — they are gone forever. Dodos were large birds that lived on an island in the Indian Ocean. The last one was killed over 300 years ago. When the last of a particular kind of animal dies out and has not been seen in the wild for 50 years, it is classed as extinct.

why do polar bears need ice?

Polar bears hunt on the ice that covers the Arctic Ocean, so they need it to live. The bears wait for seals to come up for air at holes in the ice. Now the world is warming up and the ice is melting, polar bears find it more difficult to catch food and are becoming rare.

Polar bear

Bird thief!
Many birds are rare in the wild because their eggs or chicks are stolen from their nests. The chicks are often sold as pets.

which porpoise might disappear?

The vaquita, the smallest type of porpoise, is in danger of disappearing. There are less than 250 of these shy animals left. Vaquitas are often drowned in fishing nets or killed by boats. Pollution is also a danger to them.

Vaquita

Paint
The polar bear's favourite food is seals. Paint a picture of your favourite food.

Broad-headed snake

Are there any rare snake species?

There are many rare snakes all over the world. In the United States, the large eastern indigo is a threatened species, and in Australia numbers of the broad-headed snake are dropping. The rarest snake in the UK is the smooth snake.

Smooth snake

Eastern indigo snake

345

where do lemurs live?

Lemurs live on an island called Madagascar, which is cut off from the rest of the world. They are found nowhere else in the wild and are becoming rare. If people don't protect them, they will become extinct.

Ring-tailed lemur

Draw
Imagine you are an explorer visiting an island. Draw a rare animal that lives there.

which snail was wiped out?

The partula snail was wiped out after people took a killer snail to some islands in the South Pacific Ocean. They wanted it to eat the giant African snails that were destroying crops but it ate partula snails instead.

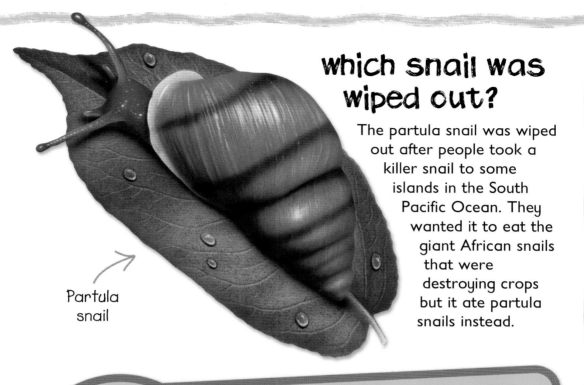

Partula snail

celebrity for two days!

People thought that solenodons had died out on the island of Cuba, but one was suddenly found! It was studied for two days and released back into the wild.

Do tigers have pouches?

No they don't! However there was a pouched animal called the Tasmanian tiger, or thylacine. They were called tigers because of their striped coats. Due to hunting, disease and the loss of its home, it is now extinct.

why did people hunt whales?

Whales were once hunted for their bones and fatty blubber. Even the fringed plates in their mouths were used to make umbrellas and tennis rackets. The northern right whale has never recovered from being hunted.

Northern right whale →

Do seals wear fur coats?

Northern fur seals have thick, soft fur, which was once used to make fur coats. Sadly, many were killed and their numbers dropped.

Discover

Find out how much a blue whale weighs when it is born. How much did you weigh as a baby?

Tangled underwater!

Dolphins may get tangled up in fishing nets. If they become trapped underwater, they will drown.

which whales are rare?

Despite being protected from hunters, seven out of the 13 great whales are still endangered. These are the humpback whale, blue whale, bowhead whale, fin whale, northern right whale, sei whale and sperm whale.

Humpback whale

Which dragon is in danger?

The leafy sea dragon. This strange animal isn't actually a dragon — it is a fish! Its leaf-like body makes it look like seaweed and helps it to hide from its enemies. They are rare because people collect them to keep as pets or make medicines.

Leafy sea dragon ↙

Hide

Dress as a leafy sea dragon and try to blend into the background. Can anyone find you?

Strange soup!

Millions of sharks are killed just for their fins, which are used to make shark fin soup. Sharks are the rarest group of animals in the oceans.

Can fish live in caves?

A fish called the Devil's Hole pupfish can. It lives in a small pool at the bottom of a cave, in a North American desert. They struggle with floods, earthquakes and changing water levels, but people are helping them to survive.

Devil's Hole pupfish

Should wild fish be kept as pets?

If fish are taken from the wild to be kept as pets, they may become rare in their natural home. If you set up a fish tank, it is best to choose common fish, which have never lived in the wild.

Are giant tortoises rare?

Yes – all giant tortoises live on just a few islands. They are rare because tourists have disturbed them and passed on diseases. People have also brought cats and rats to the islands, which eat the giant tortoises' eggs.

Galapagos giant tortoise

which frog can't croak?

The world's rarest frog, Hamilton's frog, can't croak. Unlike other frogs, it doesn't have webbed feet and it hatches from its egg as a tiny frog, instead of as a tadpole.

Hamilton's frog

Turtle tears!

The noise and bright lights of beach hotels and bars can disturb rare green turtles and stop them laying eggs.

Pretend

Put a basket on your back and see what it's like to carry your home like a giant tortoise!

why do salamanders need clean water?

Chinese and Japanese giant salamanders take in water through their skin and mouths. If the streams where they live are polluted, the salamanders take in the dirty water. This can make them ill and many may die.

why are vultures in trouble?

Long-billed vulture

Vultures are nature's very own clean-up crew. They feed on the dead bodies of farm animals, which stops them rotting away and spreading diseases. Millions of vultures have died because a drug used to treat the farm animals is poisonous to the birds.

Feed

Ask an adult to help you put out bird food, such as seeds and nuts.

Why are parrots in danger?

Parrots are the most endangered birds. They are trapped illegally and sold as pets, and the forests where they live are being cut down. About one-third of all kinds of parrot are in danger.

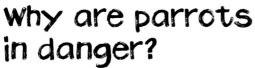

vanishing birds!

About one in every eight types of bird are in danger of becoming extinct. This means that about 1200 kinds of birds are likely to disappear in the coming years.

Scarlet macaw

which bird is a good gardener?

In the rainforests of Australia, southern cassowaries spread the seeds of plants. The birds eat the plants, and the seeds come out in their droppings around the forest.

why are pandas in peril?

Less than 2000 giant pandas live in the bamboo forests of China. The forests are being cut down by people to build farms and roads. Pandas only eat bamboo, so they can't move to other forests.

Giant pandas

Ferret families!

In 1987, wild black-footed ferrets were nearly extinct. Over 7000 babies have been born since, bringing them back from the danger of extinction.

Pygmy hog

What is a pygmy hog?

The pygmy hog is the smallest, rarest pig. It was thought to be extinct, but a small number were saved and hundreds now live in a wildlife reserve. Baby hogs born in zoos are being released into the reserve.

Visit

Take a trip to a zoo or wildlife park with your family. Do any endangered animals live there?

Which hairy Australian needs protection?

The northern hairy-nosed wombat is very rare because its grassland home has been taken over by cattle. The last few live behind a tall fence, which protects them from dingos (wild dogs), which hunt them.

why are jaguars special?

Because they are beautiful and rare! Jaguars are the biggest cats in the Americas. Even though they are protected, they are still hunted by people and their forest homes are being cut down.

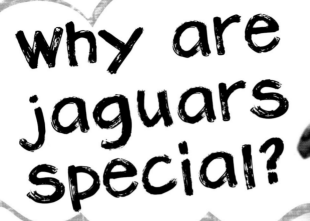

Jaguar

which cat is the fastest?

The cheetah is the fastest land animal over short distances. It cannot run at top speed for long because it gets too hot! Cheetahs are running out of space to live and may disappear.

Cheetah

Paint

Using face paints, draw stripes or spots on your face. Walk on all fours and pretend to be a tiger or a cheetah!

Tigers in trouble!

About 100 years ago, there were probably more than 100,000 tigers in the world. Now there are only 3200 and their numbers are falling rapidly.

what is the rarest cat?

The world's rarest cat is the Spanish, or Iberian, lynx. Its home has been destroyed and the rabbits it eats have been killed by diseases. There may be only about 100 of these beautiful cats left in the wild.

which ape is the most endangered?

Orang-utans are the most endangered apes. Much of their forest home has been cut down. Huge areas of palm oil plants have replaced the trees, but the orang-utans can't live there.

Orang-utans

Save the animals!

If the forests where orang-utans live are protected, it will help thousands of other animals to survive as well. All forest animals depend on each other for survival.

HOW can we help our chimp cousins?

Chimpanzees are probably the animal most closely related to us. To help them survive, wild nature reserves have been set up to protect them from hunters.

Chimp

Make

Look at the chimp picture on this page and make a cardboard chimp face mask. Your mask will need big ears!

who guards gorillas?

Rare mountain gorillas are guarded by wardens in a national park in Africa, but this is dangerous work. The wardens may be injured or killed trying to save the last few wild mountain gorillas from hunters.

why are rhinos rare?

Rhinos are rare because hunters kill them illegally and sell their horns. The horns are used to make traditional medicines or handles for daggers. Wars and the loss of their natural homes also cause trouble for rhinos.

Rhinos

what is a kouprey?

A kouprey, or grey ox, is a type of wild cattle that lives in the forests of Southeast Asia. Its numbers have fallen as low as perhaps 100, mainly because of hunting.

Kouprey

Think

Elephants are not the only animals with tusks. Can you think of a sea animal that has tusks?

Blackbuck pie!

Blackbuck antelope are doing so well on ranches in the USA that numbers have to be reduced! They are eaten in restaurants, and some are sent to India to increase numbers in the wild.

why are elephants in danger?

Elephants used be hunted for their valuable ivory tusks, and numbers are now half of what they were 30 years ago. Now the main problem is finding enough space for these huge animals to live alongside people.

Are mountain gorillas safe?

Even though there are now over 700 mountain gorillas left in the wild, these gentle apes are still on the brink of extinction. They only live in one small area of Africa and are in danger from hunters and wars near their home.

Mountain
gorilla

can tourists help endangered animals?

Tourists can pay to watch and photograph animals in the wild. This money can be used to help save animals, such as cheetahs, from extinction. Organized safaris are one great way to get close to rare animals.

Cheetah

Long gone

Humans have hunted some animals to extinction. The last great auk (a large-beaked, black-and-white sea bird) was killed in the 1850s and the species is now lost forever.

Remember

Now you have read this book, see if you can remember the names of six endangered animals.

which pigeon has gone forever?

Flocks of passenger pigeons once lived in North America. However millions of birds were shot and trapped, and their grassland homes were turned into farmland. Now passenger pigeons are extinct.

Quiz time

Do you remember what you have read about endangered animals? Here are some questions to test your memory. The pictures will help you. If you get stuck, read the pages again.

3. Why do polar bears need ice?

page 344

4. Where do lemurs live?

page 346

1. Do eagles need our help?

page 341

5. Do seals wear fur coats?

page 349

2. Can we save the dodo?

page 343

page 350

6. Which dragon is in danger?

7. Which frog can't croak?

page 353

11. How can we help our chimp cousins?

page 361

8. Why are parrots in danger?

page 355

12. Why are rhinos rare?

page 362

13. Which pigeon has gone forever?

page 365

9. Which hairy Australian needs protection?

page 357

10. Why are jaguars special?

page 358

Answers

1. Yes, because they are having trouble surviving
2. No, they are gone forever
3. They hunt on the ice, so they need it to live
4. On an island called Madagascar
5. No, but northern fur seals' fur was once used to make coats
6. The leafy sea dragon
7. Hamilton's frog
8. Because they are trapped illegally and sold as pets, and the forests where they live are being cut down
9. The northern hairy-nosed wombat
10. Because they are beautiful and rare
11. By setting up wild nature reserves to protect them from hunters
12. Because hunters kill them illegally and sell their horns
13. The passenger pigeon

index

C

H

Q

R

turtles 105, 297, 312, 316
tusks 229, 239, 280, 285, 363
Tyrannosaurus rex 342

U

UK 345
unicorns 73
urchins 316
USA 345, 363

V

vaccinations 35, 54
vaquitas 345
venom 107, 241, 282, 283, 285, 299, 314

vets 35, 43, 54, 227
Virginia opossums 117
vultures 354

W

walking 77, 81, 80, 109, 165, 229
walruses 285
warmbloods, horses 82
warrens 108
wars, animals used in 87, 237, 245, 362, 364
washing 205
Washoe (chimpanzee) 255
wasps 123, 285
water 48, 55, 58, 91, 225, 232, 240, 243, 263, 271, 274
waterholes 232, 233, 241
webs 301
whale sharks 331

whales 100, 111, 281, 348, 349
whiskers 58, 63
white tigers 196
whitetip reef sharks 317
wild cats 41, 45, 47, 52
wild dogs 12, 13, 18
wild horses 78, 93, 95
wildebeest 204, 296
wildlife parks and reserves 357, 361
wings 131
winter 174, 175
witches 45
wobbegong sharks 317
wolves 12, 295
woolly mammoths 220, 221
World Wide Fund for Nature (WWF) 183
worms 317, 321
wrasses 330, 331, 335
wrinkles 21

Y

Z

Acknowledgements

All artwork from the Miles Kelly Artwork Bank

The publishers would like to thank the following sources for the use of their photographs:

Corbis Page 152–153 Paul A. Souders

Dreamstime.com 3 Olga Khoroshunova 4 & 36(tr) Lilun; 64 Cvrgrl; 78 Fanfo; 115 Steve Byland; 121 Drpramodb; 162 giant panda: Hungchungchih, American black bear: Hilbell, sun bear: Petrmasek, spectacled bear: Starper, polar bear: F2, sloth bear: Mvshiv, moon bear: Karelgallas; 165 Pakra1k974; 169 Oksanaphoto; 171 Loflo69; 173 Anankkml; 281 Suerob; 285 Kletr; 321 Johnandersonphoto; 327 Goodolga; 329 Naluphoto

FLPA 259 Pete Oxford/Minden Pictures; 365 Ariadne Van Zandbergen

Fotolia.com 18 jsatt83; 19(b) & 36(cr) Carola Schubbel; 41 Willee Cole; 45 Fragles; 49 iChip; 60 Mr Flibble; 74(c) Jürgen Hust, (r) Bernd Meiseberg; 75(r) Linda Macpherson; 82(l) Tan Kian Khoon, (rb) Sven Cramer; 150 Fabrice Beauchene; 203 Judy Whitton; 236 TMAX; 239 Bhupi; 245 granitepeaker; 310 Desertdiver; 315 cbpix

Getty 240 Barcroft Media via Getty Images

iStockphoto.com 24 David Schliepp; 57 Tony Campbell; 62 Vladimir Suponev; 74(l) Leah-Anne Thompson; 75(l) Claudia Steininger; 76 james boulette; 122 hilton123; 137(r) Erlend Kvalsvik; 160 John Pitcher; 163 Klaas Lingbeek-van Kranen; 182 Michel de Nijs; 252 Robert Churchill; 274 Matthew Okimi; 335 Boris Tarasov; 344 Jan Will; 364 Christine Eichin

Movie Store Collection 142–143 Warner Bros. Pictures, Kingdom Feature Productions, Animal Logic, Kennedy Miller Productions; 233 Walt Disney Productions; 271 Walt Disney Productions

Naturepl.com 185 Eric Baccega

Photolibrary.com 144–145 Gerard Lacz

Rex Features 19(t) c.W. Disney/Everet; 94; 312 c.W. Disney/Everett/Rex Features

Shutterstock Cover (butterfly) hagit berkovich, (lion cub) mlorenz, (frog) Brandon Alms, (parrot) Tracy Starr, (lemur)17 plavevski; 9 Marcel Jancovic; 35 aspen rock; 43 Alberto Pérez Veiga; 46 hagit berkovich; 54 Monkey Business; 70–71 Eric Isselée; 73 Laura Gangi Pond; 82(rt) Kondrashov MIkhail Evgenevich; 81 mariait; 100–101 Kitch Bain; 103 tratong; 104 THP/Tim Hester Photography; 105 Benjamin Albiach Galan; 107 Kane513; 109 Meewezen Photography; 118 Hedrus; 130–131 Eric Isselée; 134–135 Rich Lindie; 138–139 Steve Estvanik; 139 Karel Gallas; 143 Gentoo Multimedia Ltd; 148 lfstewart; 155 Armin Rose; 191 Igor Zakowski; 197 loriklaszlo; 199 Chris Kruger; 205 Leksele; 208 palko72; 222 Josep Pena Llorens; 225 Four Oaks; 232 Igor Janicek; 233 Johan Swanepoel; 235 Carole Castelli; 241 Igor Zakowski; 251 javarman; 253 Vladimir Wrangel; 255 Sara Robinson; 260 Vitaly Titov & Maria Sidelnikova; 267 Animal; 268 Mike Price; 282 Maria Dryfhout; 287 fivespots; 291 John Arnold; 295 Tom Tietz; 297 Faiz Zaki; 299 Jubal Harshaw; 301 Steve Noakes; 302 Uryadnikov Sergey; 313 bernd.neeser; 318 Rich Carey; 322 Levent Konuk; 324 A Cotton Photo; 331 tubuceo; 333 John A. Anderson; 349 Sam Chadwick; 350 Oleksii Abramov; 355 worldswildlifewonders; 358 Karen Givens; 360–361 Eric Gevaert

Topfoto 242 The Granger Collection

All other photographs are from: digitalSTOCK, digitalvision, John Foxx, PhotoAlto, PhotoDisc, PhotoEssentials, PhotoPro, Stockbyte

Every effort has been made to acknowledge the source and copyright holder of each picture. Miles Kelly Publishing apologizes for any unintentional errors or omissions.